Seychelles.
Discovering the Economy, Governance, People and Tourism.

Author
Noah Atkinson.

Publisher
by
SONITTEC PUBLICATION.
2162 Davenport House, 261 Bolton Road.
Bury. Lancashire. BL8 2NZ. United
Kingdom

Copyright Policy

Content

Seychelles

Introduction

The Seychelles is a stable democracy with presidential and parliamentary elections held once every five years.

In the relatively short history of the Seychelles Islands, it was both a French and British colony. It gained the status of Crown colony in 1903 and by 1976 became an independent Republic with Sir James Mancham as its first democratically elected President. However in 1977, Mancham was deposed and his then Prime Minister France Albert René became President. Under President René's leadership Seychelles was a one-party

Socialist Republic state. The multi-party system in Seychelles was restored only in the mid-1990's.

In 2004, after 27 years as President, France Albert René handed over the presidency to his Vice President Jame Alix Michel. President James Michel was formally elected into office in 2006 and re-elected in 2011.

Of the country's notable achievements- Seychelles ranks Very High and is first in Africa in terms of Human Development Index (HDI was 0. 806 in 2012)

The World Bank's Worldwide Governance Indicators show that in most dimensions of governance (political stability, government effectiveness, rule of law and control of corruption), Seychelles is above the 50 percentile rank amongst the 212 countries surveyed in 2009. The 2010 Mo Ibrahim Index of African Governances shows that between 2008 and 2009, Seychelles improved its score from 77. 0 to 78. 5 (out of 100).

Geography

Located in the Indian Ocean north-east of Madagascar and 1600 km east of Kenya, the Seychelles archipelago is group of 115 granitic and coralline islands, many of which are uninhabited.

Seychelles has a total area of 455 km² making it the smallest country in Africa. The principal islands are Mahé, Praslin, and La Digue.

The Amirantes, Farquhar and Aldabra group of islands are corral islands and the UNESCO World Heritage site Aldabra is the world's largest raised coral atoll.

Coastal temperatures remain fairly constant at about 27°C throughout the year but humidity levels tend to remain high. High winds and extreme weather patterns are rare, however heavy rainfall and flooding have known to occur after tropical storms in the neighboring regions.

Demographics

In 2012, the population of Seychelles was estimated at 88303. The mainland of Mahe is the most populated with more than 90% of the population living on Mahe and followed by Praslin and La Digue.

The islands' history has a notable impact on the island natives. Seychelloise are usually of mixed descent of the original French, African, Indian and Chinese settlers and also include those who have immigrated to the islands.

Christianity is the most predominant religion with nearly 88% Roman Catholics. There are minority religions that practice Hinduism, Islam, Bahai' and other teachings. The official languages are English, French and Seychellois Creole which has its roots tied to French and other African dialects.

Economy

Alt text for sample image

The main pillars of the Seychelles' economy are tourism and fishing. The tourism sector employs about 30% of the labour force, however global trends play a critical role in the steady influx of visitors. Thus, the Government is encouraging the small population to branch out into other sectors including Offshore banking, farming and small-scale manufacturing.

The public sector drives the economy and accounts for more than 40% of GDP. The government controls the importation, licensing and distribution of virtually all goods and services and exercises significant control over all sectors of the economy. However, in 2005 and 2006 it implemented several measures aimed at liberalising trade and privatising state-owned entities.

Seychelles exports canned tuna, frozen fish, cinnamon bark, copra and petroleum products. It imports machinery and equipment, foodstuffs, petroleum products and chemicals. Its major trading partners are United Kingdom, France, Spain, Japan, Italy, Germany, Saudi Arabia, Singapore and South Africa. The currency of Seychelles is the Seychellois rupee (SCR).

Despite having one of the highest per capita incomes in Africa, Seychelles is vulnerable economically, due to its small size, isolation, limited natural resources and dependence on tourism, which accounts for the bulk of foreign-exchange earnings. Though tourism worldwide grew strongly during the 1990s, and cheaper long-haul flights made destinations such as Seychelles more accessible, the industry became increasingly competitive. Imports needed for tourism were in large part responsible for the country's trade deficit. GDP grew by 1. 4 per cent p. a. 1979–89.

Consequently, the government made efforts to diversify the economy, encouraging farming, fishing and manufacturing in the whole country including the outer islands. State-owned and parastatal enterprises accounted in the mid-1990s for more than half of GDP and some privatisation of state enterprises was under way during the 1990s. By the late 1990s, there was good growth for several years, and canned tuna became the major export.

But the economy underwent a small overall decline during 2001–04, before growth strengthened to seven to ten per cent in 2005–07, as a result of increased foreign direct investment and tourism receipts. Then, in 2008, in the teeth of the world economic downturn, the economy stalled and Seychelles turned to the IMF for emergency support. With a sharp fall in tourism income and cuts in public expenditure, GDP shrank by 2. 1 per cent in 2008 and by 1. 1 per cent in 2009. However, in response to economic reforms initiated in late November 2008, in 2010–11 the economy bounced back, with two years of strong growth, followed by good steady growth in 2012–15.

History

Although visited by Phoenicians, Malays and Arabs, and used in the 16th century by the Portuguese as a stopover point, the Seychelles remained largely uninhabited until the 17th century.

Pirates and privateers set up bases on the islands and in 1741 the Governor of Mauritius (then called Île de France) sent Lazare Picault to explore them. The French claimed possession of the islands in 1756 and French settlers from Mauritius, with their African slaves, began to arrive from 1770.

British attempts to take possession in the late 18th century were confounded by the pacifying tactics of Governor Queau de Quinssy, who several times surrendered to British aggressors, then after their departure, raised the French flag again. After the Napoleonic Wars, by the Treaty of Paris (1814), the Seychelles was ceded to Britain, together with Mauritius. From then until 1903, it was administered from Mauritius.

The Seychelles had long provided a transit point for slaves from Africa. Britain abolished trade in slaves at the beginning of the 19th century (abolishing slavery itself in 1834) and British vessels were active in attacking Spanish, Arab and other slaving vessels. About 3,000 Africans rescued from Arab slave traders on the East African coast between 1861 and 1874 were removed to Seychelles, to become labourers on the plantations. The British also exiled some West African chiefs, who were continuing to resist British control, to Seychelles. There was also some Chinese and Indian settlement in the 19th century, most commonly by traders.

Poverty was widespread by 1918, due partly to a fall in vanilla prices (an artificial substitute having been discovered). New cash crops such as cinnamon and copra were then introduced. In the

1940s, the Association of Seychelles Taxpayers protested against the UK's management of the islands. In 1964 the Seychelles Democratic Party (SDP), led by James Mancham, and the Seychelles People's United Party (SPUP), led by France Albert René, were founded. The SDP favoured retaining close ties with the UK; the SPUP campaigned for autonomy.

Universal adult suffrage was introduced in 1967, for elections of members of the legislative council. The council became a 15-member legislative assembly in 1970 (later National Assembly) and general elections were held in which the SDP won six seats and the SPUP five. Mancham became chief minister. At the next elections in 1974, the SDP won 52% of the votes, the SPUP 47%; Seychelles achieved internal self-government in the following year.

Parliament then voted for independence, a new constitution was finalised in 1976, and Seychelles became an independent republic within the Commonwealth. Mancham became president and René prime minister.

At independence Mancham and the SDP's policies favoured development based on tourism and offshore financial services and alignment with the West, whereas René and the SPUP wanted a non-aligned policy and the development of a selfreliant economy centred on nationalised industry. The SPUP staged an armed coup in June 1977, while Mancham was in the UK attending a Commonwealth summit and Seychelles became a socialist state, with René as its president and the SPUP, renamed the Seychelles People's Progressive Front (SPPF), the sole political party. There was extensive nationalisation of enterprises, including hotels and industries.

There were a number of threatened coup plots against the René government, the most serious in 1981, when about 50 mercenaries, recruited in South Africa, attempted a landing in Mahé. When their weapons were discovered at the airport, the mercenaries escaped by hijacking an Air India jet, leaving five of their number behind.

However, opposition from exiled political supporters of the SDP and Mancham continued throughout the 1980s, and was reinforced by the turning of the international tide against centralised economic control and one-party rule towards the end of the decade. By 1990, opposition within the country also became vocal, and the government began to consider the need for change.

In December 1991, the government passed legislation to provide for multiparty democracy. Eight parties were registered by July 1992, and a constitutional commission elected to prepare a new constitution which paved the way for presidential and legislative elections in July 1993. René took 59% of votes in the presidential election and Sir James Mancham 36%; and the SPPF gained a large majority 27 of the 33 seats in the National Assembly.

In the March 1998 elections, President René (with 67% of the votes) was returned and his SPPF won 24 of the 25 Assembly seats (30 of 34 when seats allocated on a proportional basis were included). Mancham (14%) was overtaken by Wavel

Ramkalawan of the United Opposition party (19%) as opposition leader.

History of Politics in the Seychelles

French rule

The political history of Seychelles started when the islands were first discovered and colonized by the French. The year was 1742 and a group of 28 men and women (mainly African slaves and French settlers) landed on the small island of St Anne to start what is now known as the Seychellois nation. For more than half a century, the French occupied the main islands of Mahe, Praslin, La Digue and Silhouette. The other 100 islands or so, the outer coralline islands remained more or less uninhabited except for passing ships looking for timber and water. Seychelles lying off the coast of eastern African had become an important colony for the African slaves and a frequent stop-over for food and water for passing ships. Seychelles got its name after the Jean Moreau de Sechelles, who was a French Finance Minister during the reign of Louis XV.

British rule

In 1804 Seychelles became a British Colony. The name Sechelles was changed to Seychelles. Between 1811 and 1888 Seychelles was administered by Mauritius. In 1889 Seychelles saw its first legislative council following a semi-separation from Mauritius when the Constitution changed in 1888 to allow for a local Administrator. In 1903 the first executive and legislative council of Seychelles, then a crown colony, was born. Seychellois representation at the level of the council was non-existent. A small number of people were nominated by the governor to the Council.

Political party elections

The first election of universal adult suffrage took place in 1967 which then formed the colonial Legislative Council. The 1967 election had followed the formation of two parties in 1964, first the Seychelles People's United Party (SPUP) under the direction of France Albert Rene and the Seychelles Democratic Party (SDP) headed by

James Mancham. SPUP was advocating Independence, SDP was against it. The 1967 the Governing Council was comprised of eight members, (3 SPUP, 4 SDP, 1 Independent). During that election Dr. Marie Hilda Stevenson-Delhomme also become the first woman parliamentarian.

Pre independence years

The pre-independence years were marked by a series of elections all in the run-up to the independence. The SDP in majority campaigned for Seychelles to remain a British colony, the SPUP fought for independence. But the first apparent move for Seychelles to gain independence came through a motion by James Mancham calling on a change in the Constitution by the British government.

In 1970, a Constitutional Conference was held in Marlborough House which effected in some important changes in the Constitution. Following the changes, the Governing Council became the Legislative Assembly and its number of representations was increased from 8 to fifteen. It also marked the introduction for the concept of separation of powers. The constitutional change had effectively changed the political system into that of a ministerial government which marked a separation between the executive and the legislative.

The 1970 election which preceded the changes saw a new Legislative Assembly with for the first time a speaker, Mr. Michel Lousteau-Lalanne. In 1974, the Legislative Assembly tabled a motion calling for the country's Independence. 1975 saw the formation of a coalition government, the first semblance of an internal self government. In short, the first steps towards independence. The institution's name also changed from Legislative Assembly into House of Assembly. In January 1976 a meeting of the Constitutional Conference in Marlborough House officially set the date for the country's independence to June 29th 1976.

The first republic

On June 29th 1976, Seychelles officially became the Republic of Seychelles. A new country was born and so was a new era in Seychelles' politics. The first republic which lasted for little less than a year saw for the first time the use of the term National Assembly to refer to the legislature. For the first time, Seychelles was also headed by a President, James Mancham and the leader of the House, was Prime Minister France Albert Rene.

The first republic was also an important period in our political history as it marked an era of self discovery and self rule. Seychelles had just become a republic, considered to be a small and poor African nation. The newly born Seychelles was also a shaky one, headed by a coalition government with different ideologies of governance. It is to be noted that the first amendment to the Independent Constitution was one asking for a policy of bilingualism, a call for both French and English to be used as an administrative language.

The second republic

For two years following the June 1977 Coup d'état, the country was ruled by decree as any form of legislature was suspended.

A year later in 1978, a Constitutional Council appointed a new Constitution, and the second republic was born. In 1979, during the one party era, a new legislature came into being, named at the time, the People's Assembly.

The second republic which saw four elections went through different constitutional changes, including the establishment of the one party state, the increase in electoral districts, and most importantly was a move away from the standard Westminster system adopted in several commonwealth countries. The People's Assembly was presided by the Chairman and government Ministers came to answer questions put by the district's representatives and for bills. This was the first semblance for the legislature to operate on a separate platform than that of the government, and for the first time the People's Assembly had a separate secretariat.

In 1992, during an SPPF congress, former President Rene announced the return of a multi party system of governance. The preparatory phase for that to happen first stated with an election for the people of Seychelles to decide who would represent them at the Constitutional Commission, the body that was to draft the constitution for the third republic. The results came in, SPPF had 14 representatives and the DP, eight. Other smaller parties which had been formed by then, six of them, did not muster enough support and the 5% requirement that was needed to form part of the commission.

For several months, opinion leaders and experts, most notably church and political leaders from all corners of the islands, had their say in what should be the Constitution of Seychelles. The first referendum failed to reach the 60% requirement for the constitution to be adopted. A second round of negotiations between the two main parties resumed in January 1993 and the deliberations were broadcast in its entirety on national television and radio. It is interesting to note that the process became a very public one, with greater interests of the population not only through their tuning in to their TV sets every evening to watch the sometimes comic deliberations, but on a more serious level, to submit their views and contributions. On June 18, 1993 the people of Seychelles supported the new Constitution with a resounding 73. 9%. June 18th was then declared the National Day for the republic of Seychelles.

Multi-party democracy The third republic

In his book, a Parliamentary History of Seychelles, the former Speaker of the National Assembly, Judge Francis Macgregor, called the early days a "pioneer" parliament. That he did for very valid reasons. For the first time, the National Assembly building had to move to the then newly built National Library building. Before that the business of the house was in a small hall at National House. "It was very much a pioneer parliament in trying to cultivate a workable body in a climate of inevitably necessary dialogue and tolerance, the nation having just gone through the equivalent of five general elections, in the space of less than two years. We had to sit with, work with and live with each other with the responsibility of making this new Seychelles work"

The Seychelles was officially separated from the territory of Mauritius and became a British Crown Colony in 1903; in 1976, the islands became a independent republic within the British Commonwealth. However, in 1977, a coup overthrew the republic's first president, James Mancham, and installed a socialist administration run by two men over the next few decades: France Albert René from 1977 through 2004, James Michel from 2004 to the present. A constitution essentially mandating socialism and a one-party system was proclaimed in 1979 and lasted until 1991; a new replacement constitution allowing opposition parties was not put into effect, however, until it was approved in 1993 by the island's voters.

Organization of the Seychelles Government

The President of the Seychelles is both the head of the government and the head of state. Selection of the President is by popular vote in an election held every five years. No opposition candidate ran for President until the elections of 1994. The government headed by the President wields executive power through an appointed cabinet. Legislative power is based in the National Assembly, twenty-five of whose members are elected to five-year terms by popular vote in specific constituencies, with the remaining nine out of the thirty-four seats appointed by the government based on a proportional formula allocating those seats to members of political parties by the percentage of votes in the election for that party. The membership of the President's cabinet must be approved by the National Assembly.

There are twenty-five administrative regions that form the constituencies of the National Assembly. The collection of eight districts that comprise the capital city on the main island of Mahé is called Greater Victoria; the remainder of the rural areas on the island of Mahé comprise another fourteen districts. Two more districts are on the island of Praslin; the district based on the island of La Digue includes some other smaller nearby islands. All the other Outer Islands do not belong to any district and have no distinct representation in the National Assembly.

Current State of Political Parties in the Seychelles

As of 2012, there are two political parties in the Seychelles, the ruling People's Party (PP) and the opposition Seychelles National Party (SNP). In the last national election in 2007, the People's Party won well over fifty per cent of the popular vote, which continued the incumbent James Michel in the office of President. The People's Party acquired twenty-three out of the thirty-four seats available in the National Assembly as a result of that same election. The next national election is scheduled for the spring of 2012.

The People's Party

The history of the People's Party stretches back to 1964, when the Seychelles was still a British colony. At that time, the organization, then known as the Seychelles People's United Party (SPUP) and led by France-Albert Rene, opposed British colonial rule and advocated the creation of an independent socialist government in the Seychelles. In 1977, this group changed its name to Seychelles People's Progressive Front (SPPF) and ran the coup that overthrew the President installed upon independence from Britain in the previous year. In 2009, this political organization changed its name to the People's Party. The SPUP/SPPF/PP has ruled the Seychelles since 1977, winning every national presidential election, though the opposition SNP claims the buying of votes has been a major factor in those victories.

The National Party

The SNP, the current opposition party in the Seychelles, has its roots in the 1990s when the constitution approved in 1993 allowed opposition candidates to run in national elections. At that time, three political parties opposed the rule of President René, at that time having continually been in power for sixteen years:

✓ *the Seychelles National Movement, with leader Gérard Hoarau*

✓ *the National Alliance Party, with leader Philippe Boullé*

✓ *the Parti Seselwa, with leader Wavel Ramkalawan.*

These three political parties merged in 1994 to from the Seychelles National Party with Ramkalawan, a priest in the Anglican faith, as its leader. In recent elections, Ramkalawan, acquiring between 42-46% of the presidential vote, has come in a close second to the ruling party's candidate. In the current National Assembly, the SNP now holds seven seats by constituency vote and four seats by the proportional appointment rule for a total of eleven seats out of the thirty-four total. The SNP is considered a liberal party, emphasizing economic reforms, democracy based on multiple political parties and an official respect for individual rights.

International Reputation of the Seychelles Government

Despite what the situation may appear from the above description of internal politics, the current government of the Seychelles ranks second only to Mauritius in the Ibrahim Index of African Governance, a ranking on the excellence of government operations as it pertains to the delivery of essential goods, services and basic rights to its citizens. The index covers all forty-eight sub-Saharan nations, ranking them in many different ways and including such categories as Human Development, Human Rights and Safety/Security. In addition, the Seychelles actively participates in such global organizations as the British Commonwealth of Nations, La Francophonie and the Indian Ocean Commission.

Society

Population:

93,000 (2013); 88 per cent on Mahé, seven per cent on Praslin, three per cent on La Digue and two per cent on the other islands, with 53 per cent living in urban areas; growth 1. 3 per cent p. a. 1990–2013; birth rate 17 per 1,000 people; life expectancy 73 years.

The population is of mixed African, French, Indian, Chinese and Arab descent. There are small minorities of Europeans, Indians and Chinese.

Language:

The official languages are Creole, English and French. Seychellois Creole (Kreol Seselwa) is French-based and very widely used.

Religion:

Mainly Christians (Roman Catholics 76 per cent, Anglicans six per cent, and small numbers of other Christians); Hindus two per cent and Muslims one per cent (2010 census). Belief in the supernatural and gris-gris (the old magic of spirits) often coexists with Christian and other beliefs. Sorcery was outlawed in 1958.

Health:

Public spending on health was four per cent of GDP in 2012. A network of polyclinics provides general medical care, dentistry and other services. There are also private general practitioners. The public health service depends heavily on medical personnel from overseas. There is no malaria, yellow fever or bilharzia. Some 96 per cent of the population uses an improved drinking water source and 97 per cent have access to adequate sanitation facilities (2012). Infant mortality was 12 per 1,000 live births in 2013 (43 in 1978).

Education:

Public spending on education was four per cent of GDP in 2011. There are ten years of compulsory education starting at the age of six. Primary school comprises six years and secondary five, with cycles of three and two years. Some 94 per cent of pupils complete primary school (2010). The school year starts in January. Teaching is in Creole, French and English.

The Seychelles Polytechnic opened in January 1983 at Anse Royale on the island of Mahé. It offers courses in business and the visual arts to diploma level and has been providing first-year degree courses in conjunction with the University of Manchester, UK, since 2001. The Seychelles Institute of Technology was established in Providence, Mahé, in 2005–06, incorporating the technical studies programmes of the polytechnic. Other important tertiary institutions include the National Institute of Education, National Institute for Health and Social Studies, Agricultural and Horticultural Training Centre, Maritime Training Centre and Seychelles Tourism Academy. The female–male ratio for gross enrolment in tertiary education is 3. 40:1 (2011). Literacy among people aged 15–24 is 99 per cent (2010).

Media:

The Rising Sun and Seychelles Nation (state-owned) are published daily. Weeklies include Le Nouveau Seychelles, The People (owned by the People's Party) and Regar (Seychelles National Party).

The Seychelles Broadcasting Corporation provides public radio and TV services in Creole, French and English. Multichannel cable and satellite TV services are also available.

Some 95 per cent of households have TV sets (2010). There are 216 personal computers per 1,000 people (2007).

Communications:

Country code 248; internet domain '. sc'. Payphones are available in most districts on the inner islands. Internet connections are good in Seychelles. There are several internet cafes on Mahé, Praslin and La Digue. The main post office is in Victoria.

For every 1,000 people there are 234 landlines, 1,473 mobile phone subscriptions and 504 internet users (2013).

Public holidays:

New Year (two days), Labour Day (1 May), Liberation Day (anniversary of the 1977 coup, 5 June), National Day (18 June), Independence Day (29 June), Assumption (15 August), All Saints' Day (1 November), Immaculate Conception (8 December) and Christmas Day. Religious festivals whose dates vary from year to year include Good Friday, Easter Monday and Corpus Christi.

Constitution and politics

The independence constitution provided for a multiparty state. The 1979 constitution made Seychelles a one-party state, the sole candidate for a presidential election to be nominated by the ruling party. This constitution was amended in 1992, when multiparty democracy was reintroduced and, after a process of consultation involving referendums, replaced by the 1993 constitution. Under the 1993 constitution,

Seychelles is a unitary republic, with a multiparty democracy. It has a unicameral parliament, the National Assembly, comprising up to 35 seats, 25 of which are elected by universal adult suffrage, on a first-past-the-post basis, and up to ten seats on the basis of proportional representation. Parliamentary and presidential elections take place every five years, not necessarily at the same time. The president appoints a cabinet not including members of parliament and is empowered under the 1993 constitution to rule by decree. In August 1996, the constitution was amended to create the office of vice-president.

Politics

Following the 1998 elections Wavel Ramkalawan formed a new party, the Seychelles National Party (SNP), to succeed his United Opposition party. In an early presidential election in September 2001, René was returned to office, securing 54 per cent of the votes, defeating Ramkalawan (45 per cent), in a much closer contest than in 1998. Though the SNP significantly strengthened its position in the parliamentary elections in December 2002, with 11 of the 34 elective seats and 43 per cent of the votes, the ruling Seychelles People's Progressive Front (SPPF) with 23 seats remained in control of the National Assembly.

Following the elections, the SPPF chose Vice-President and Finance Minister James Michel as their candidate for the presidential contest due in 2006, France Albert René being allowed only two terms under the constitution. In April 2004, after almost 27 years as head of state, René stood down and Michel became President.

Michel was endorsed by the electorate in the July 2006 presidential contest when, with 54 per cent of the votes cast, he defeated the SNP's Wavel Ramkalawan.

In the parliamentary elections held in May 2007, the ruling SPPF, with 56 per cent of the votes, again won 23 seats and the SNP, with 44 per cent, again took 11. At its 24th National Congress in June 2009 the SPPF was renamed the People's Party.

In the May 2011 presidential election Michel was re-elected, winning 56 per cent of the votes cast. His principal rival, Ramkalawan of the SNP, secured 41 per cent of the votes. A Commonwealth expert team present declared the electoral process credible. Among its recommendations were that the government carry out a thorough review of electoral legislation, and establish an independent electoral commission, as recommended in the April 2010 report of the Constitutional Review Commission.

Following the presidential election in May 2011 the SNP boycotted parliament citing the slow pace of electoral reform. Some disaffected SNP members then formed a new party, the Popular Democratic Movement (PDM), to fight the parliamentary elections which were held from 29 September to 1 October 2011. The elections were again won by the People's Party led by President James Michel, taking all 25 elective seats in the National Assembly and receiving 89 per cent of the votes cast. The PDM took 11 per cent of the votes but failed to win any of the elective seats. After the nine seats decided by proportional representation had been added, the People's Party had 33 seats and the PDM one seat in the new National Assembly. Turnout was 74 per cent, down from around 86 per cent in the last three elections.

The Electoral Commission was appointed in August 2011 and the Forum for Electoral Reform inaugurated in January 2012 with the support of all five registered political parties embarked on a series of public hearings, with a view to making recommendations on reform of election law.

Politics, government

Since achieving independence from the United Kingdom in 1976, the Seychelles political scene has been dominated by the intense competition between 2 political parties and personalities, the right-centrist Seychelles Democratic Party (SDP) and the leftist Seychelles People's United Party (SPUP). Immediately after independence, Sir James Mancham of the SDP became the first president and France Albert Rene of the SPUP became prime minister. The coalition unraveled after a 1977 coup by Rene that forced Mancham into exile. In 1979, the constitution of 1976 was replaced by a significantly revised one that replaced the multiparty system with a one-party state. The SPUP, renamed to the Seychelles People's Progressive Front (SPPF), became the only political party in the country. Rene was elected president in 1979 and survived several coup attempts. In a dramatic political turn, the one-party political system was abandoned in 1992 under a new constitution that restored multiparty rule and saw Mancham return from exile to lead the SDP once more. Support of the SDP gradually declined with the rise of another opposition party, the Seychelles National Party (SNP, formerly the United Opposition), led by Wavel Ramkalawan. In elections for the 35-seat legislature in 1998, the SPPF won 61. 7 percent of the vote, SNP won 26. 1 percent, and the SDP won only 12. 1 percent. Rene also won reelection as president. Despite this political tumult, elections and transitions of power have been peaceful.

Under President Rene, Seychelles introduced a socialist economy with state control over economic activities and 5-year national development plans, though the government also sought financial assistance from England and France. The main aims of the government policy were the diversification of the national economy, development of agricultural and manufacturing industries, the production of goods for domestic consumption and for export, and increase of hard currency. Most tax revenues in the Seychelles are derived from the net income or profit of a business. This tax is paid by resident and non-resident business owners on a graduated scale that ranges from 0 percent of the first SRe24,000 of income up to 40 percent of higher levels of income. Imported products, including alcohol and cigarettes, are also taxed. In 1998 trade taxes accounted for 44 percent of total revenues

Under the 1993 constitution, Seychelles is a unitary republic with a multiparty democracy, a unicameral parliament and an executive president who is permitted to serve for a maximum of three five-year terms.

The independence constitution provided for a multiparty state. The 1979 constitution rendered Seychelles a one-party state, the sole candidate for a presidential election to be nominated by the ruling party. This constitution was amended in 1992 when multiparty democracy was reintroduced.

Under the 1993 constitution, the president is head of state, head of government and commander-in-chief of the armed forces. The president is elected

on the basis of universal adult suffrage, and is empowered to rule by decree.

The president appoints a cabinet of between seven and 14 members not including members of parliament subject to approval of the majority in the National Assembly.

The National Assembly comprises up to 35 seats, of which 25 are elected by universal adult suffrage, on a first-past-the-post basis, and up to ten additional seats are allocated on the basis of proportional representation. Parliamentary elections take place every five years, not necessarily at the same time as the presidential elections.

In 1996 the constitution was amended to create the office of vice-president.

The 1993 constitution provides for separation of powers between the executive, legislature and judiciary. The judicial system derives from English common law and the French Napoleonic Code, and also includes elements of customary law.

The most serious civil and criminal cases, and appeals from the magistrates' courts, come before the Supreme Court. The Constitutional Court is a division of the Supreme Court and deals with human rights as well as constitutional matters. Appeals from the Supreme Court are heard by the Court of Appeal. Other courts include the rent tribunal and the industrial court.

Regional & Local Government

Seychelles has local appointed administrations which run each of the 25 districts and through which the government facilitates community-based services and agencies. Local administrations have no powers to raise revenue and are funded by the central government. The Local Government Act of 1991 was suspended in 1993 under the new constitution which allows for local administration but there are no direct constitutional provisions or relevant legislation to support this. The minister of local government within the Community Development Department (CDD), part of the Ministry for Community Development, Youth and Sports (MCDYS), is responsible for monitoring local administration in the 25 districts. In addition, district community councils were reintroduced in 1999; 12 members of each district community council are appointed by the minister of local government for two-year terms.

The councils are advisory and bring forth the expressed wishes, aspirations and day to day concerns of the community. The District Social Committee and the District Team coordinate local programmes and encourage community development work. Seychelles' 25 administrative districts comprise all of the inner islands: eight districts form the capital and are referred to as Greater Victoria, another 14 districts make up the rest of the main island of Mahé, two districts on the island of Praslin and one on La Digue. Given the lack of inhabitants in the outer islands, they do not have administrative districts or formal government.

Two new parties enter Seychelles political landscape

With the next Seychelles presidential and parliamentary elections on the horizon, the political atmosphere in the Indian Ocean archipelago of 115 islands with a population of around 90,000 people, is starting to heat up with parties and individuals starting to make known their intentions to participate in the next democratic polls.

Recently the Independent Conservative Union of Seychelles (ICUS) was registered as a new party, bringing the total to six registered political parties in the small island state, of which the socialist party 'Parti Lepep' (People's Party) is in power.

On Friday, a newly formed 'Lalyans Seselwa' [Seychellois Alliance], submitted its registration documents to the Electoral Commission, following rumours about the party's formation circulating in the islands for weeks.

After the President of Seychelles, James Michel, leader of the Parti Lepep, confirmed in February this year that he intends to run for a third term in office, the three main opposition parties in the Indian Ocean archipelago, namely: the Seychelles National Party (SNP), the Seychelles United Party (SUP) and the People's Democratic Movement (PDM) also confirmed that they would be participating. The Seychelles Freedom Party has not made any public statement.

Philippe Boullé, a Seychellois lawyer, who stood as an independent candidate in past presidential elections has also presented his manifesto for 'Change and Renaissance' earlier this month, announcing in a local newspaper that he intends to stand again as independent candidate.

Lalyans Seselwa - break-away faction from the ruling party

A press statement from 'Lalyans Selselwa' issued Friday afternoon said the application to register the party had been presented to the Chairman of the Electoral Commission, Hendrick Gappy.

"As [the] leader of our party, Lalyans Seselwa, Mr. Patrick Pillay and Secretary General Ahmed Afif have handed over all the required documents to Mr. Gappy and he has confirmed that everything is in order. The Electoral Commission will now consider the application and will subsequently inform us of its decision," added the statement.

Pillay was a high-ranking figure within the Parti Lepep, who was the islands' Minister for Foreign Affairs from 2005 to 2010 and was then posted as Seychelles High Commissioner to the UK until 2012, when he retired.

Ahmed Afif was also a high-ranking official with the Seychelles government, who served as CEO of the Seychelles International Business Authority and then later as Principal Secretary for Finance and Trade between 2007 and 2012.

The Treasurer of the Lalyans Seselwa is a wealthy Seychellois-Indian businessman, Dr. Vaithinathaswamy Ramadoss, who was previously Chairman of the Seychelles Chamber of Commerce and Industry and also Treasurer of the Parti Lepep from January to August 2012.

In an interview with daily newspaper TODAY in Seychelles on Thursday, Pillay said "it is not our opponents' weaknesses or faults which make our strength, but rather it is our beliefs, plans and vision for our cause which define us and very soon all these will be revealed to the public so that they can decide. "

In Saturday's edition of the newspaper, it was confirmed by Pillay that former government minister William Herminie, who served in various ministries between 1988-2004, as well as former government minister from 1998-2006 and Seychelles high commissioner to South Africa from 2007-2009, Noellie Alexander, are undertaking mobilisation and communication roles within the newly formed party.

Commenting on the recent development of a breakaway faction, the founding President of the Parti Lepep, France Albert Rene affirmed that he did not support the new party.

"I do not support people who conspire against the beliefs of this party. To me they are traitors to their own beliefs," he said in last week's edition of Parti Lepep's mouthpiece, 'The People'.

'Parti Lepep' was founded 50 years ago in 1964 by France Albert Rene when at the time it was known as the 'Seychelles People's United Party' (SPUP).

It became the 'Seychelles People's Progressive Front' (SPPF) in June 1978 and in June 2009 the party's name changed for a third time to what it is known as today, 'Parti Lepep'. Rene served as President of the Seychelles from 1977 until 2004, when he retired.

A conservative union with former PDM members

The Independent Conservative Union of Seychelles (ICUS), was registered by the Electoral Commission a month ago.

The ICUS's leaders have expressed their aim to take part in both the next presidential and legislative elections.

The party has Jona Alcindor as its leader, Ralph Ernesta as deputy leader and Mike Chadstone who is the party's founder, as secretary general.

Chadstone, who is also the party's spokesperson, told SNA that ICUS, whose motto is 'celebrating the birth of a new vision of hope for Seychelles' was responding to "the thirst for a new political party among the population. "

Chadstone who said he is now full-time in politics has in the past worked for the Seychelles ministry of education and most recently he was a business studies lecturer in Qatar.

"No election is easy and you cannot predict the outcome but based on the fact that we know that people are tired of the political landscape and they want something new... we find ourselves in a position where we cannot guarantee a total win, but we can make a big difference," said Chadstone.

"We are founded on democracy. One key focus is giving equal opportunities to everyone particularly women and youth to be empowered to take leadership roles, and we also have a national development plan which is for a hundred years. I will not be here in 25 years, in a hundred years, but the plan will set forth what Seychelles needs to achieve."

Alcindor, Ernesta and Chadstone told SNA that they had all intended to present their candidacy individually for the next presidential elections before joining together as ICUS and that it will not be necessarily one of them that will stand as the presidential candidate.

The party is now planning a series of preliminary elections across the country, which started Saturday April 25, for their members to choose who they want to have as their presidential candidate.

"We will go through all the districts and ask the members to nominate and vote for who they think will be a good presidential candidate. When we have been round all the districts we will have our caucus and have all candidates present their plan for Seychelles and our members will decide who came out more and have him or her as our presidential candidate...The others will be candidates for the national assembly elections," said Chadstone.

Alcindor, Ernesta and Chadstone have all been involved in politics in one way or another in the past. Chadstone was going to stand as the vice-presidential candidate of Viral Dhanjee, a Seychellois citizen who attempted to enter the 2011 presidential race, and was disqualified by the Electoral Commission for not meeting the set criteria.

Alcindor was the campaign manager for the Popular Democratic Movement (PDM) led by the leader of the opposition in the National Assembly, David Pierre, in the last legislative elections.

"It's not going to be easy but I believe we can do it...as a woman my role is to administer the party and bring it forward," Alcindor told SNA.

As for Ernesta, a businessman in the construction field, he stood as the PDM candidate in the Anse Etoile district, in the northern part of the Seychelles main island of Mahé during the same election, but did not win the majority vote.

"I enjoy democracy when people are free to express themselves. I have seized the opportunity to join ICUS because I appreciate what Mr Chadstone is putting forward," said Ernesta. "ICUS's programme will bring a better life for all Seychellois. I believe it will bring prosperity for all. My aim in politics is to help bring about a change in the country. "

No date set yet

The last presidential election in Seychelles was held in May 2011, and the parliamentary elections took place in September the same year.

According to the country's constitutional requirements, the next presidential election should be organised within 90 days after January 2016.

Local media have already begun to speculate that the head of state will take a gamble and call early presidential elections before the end of this year, which he is permitted to do according to the 5th amendment of the Seychelles constitution.

Responding to the rumours of an early election in an interview with SNA in February, Michel said he had not yet made a decision yet, adding that the matter was still "to be decided."

Michel's candidacy still needs to be officially confirmed by Parti Lepep's Congress, which according to Friday's edition of 'The People' newspaper is scheduled to take place in June

President Michel announces resignation after first election victory for the opposition in 40 years

After having dominated Seychellois politics for nearly 40 years, on September 10th the Seychelles People's Party (Parti Lepep in Creole) lost the parliamentary elections in the small Indian Ocean archipelago. The election victory of the opposition (the Seychelles Democratic Alliance Linyon Demokratik Seselwa) constitutes a dramatic political shift in the country, and can be regarded as a major step in its development towards a consolidated democracy. The recent parliamentary elections were preceded by a presidential election in December 2015, which produced a razor-thin victory (50,15% of votes) for the incumbent president, James Alix Michel. After his party's defeat in the parliamentary elections, Michel who has been president of Seychelles since 2004 announced his resignation, and his intention to hand over powers to the vice president, Danny Faure. The resignation of the 74-year old president announced via a surprise address on national television came as a major shock to the island nation.

The People's Party and its predecessor, the Seychelles Peoples Patriotic Front (SPPF), have controlled Seychellois politics for virtually the entire post-independence period. Seychelles obtained independence from the United Kingdom in 1976, but within a year after the attainment of sovereignty, the Marxist SPPF, headed by its charismatic leader France-Albert René, staged a successful coup d'état with help from socialist African countries like Libya and Tanzania. Between 1977 and 1993, Seychelles was ruled as a single-party dictatorship, and human rights abuses were commonplace. The fall of the Berlin Wall and the collapse of the Soviet Union instigated a transition to multi-party democracy, and Seychelles has been an electoral democracy since the early 1990s. However, the SPPF and René continued to win all subsequent elections, and international observers remained very critical of Seychellois democracy, highlighting the political fusion between the state and the ruling party as particularly problematic. Under René's guidance Seychelles reached an impressive level of economic growth, as a result of which it is now one of the wealthiest countries of Africa. This economic success undoubtedly contributed to the continuing support for the SPPF, also after René transferred powers to Michel in 2004, and the SPPF was transformed into the People's Party.

While the political opposition had boycotted the penultimate parliamentary elections in 2011 due to concerns about unequal campaign finance, in advance to last September's election four opposition parties joined forces in a political alliance (the Seychelles Democratic Alliance), which managed to win 19 of the 33 parliamentary seats. Since the presidency of the country remains in the hands of the People's Party, the tiny archipelago now enters a period of divided government. Both the newly designated president and the political leadership of Seychelles Democratic Alliance have declared their intention to cooperate with each other, but how this cooperation will play out in the coming years remains to be seen. While the two political parties are ideologically similar and do not have many disagreements regarding economic policies, the relationship between them has been marked by strong and sometimes personal antagonism.

Seychelles Political Freedom!

A community of decent freedom loving Seychellois,determined to see Seychelles FREE from the clutches of failure, corruption, and lack of respect of Democracy and fundamental human rights. A spin off of the anti Communist league who believe in Sesel Pou Seselwa.

The islands of the Seychelles, scattered across the Indian Ocean to the north of Madagascar, are better known for their beauty than for their political culture. But beneath the surface a political battle is raging.

Elections for the presidency of the Seychelles will be held from May 19 - 21, 2011. A Commonwealth Expert Team has been sent to observe the poll. The opposition leader, Wavel Ramkalawan, told Think

Africa Press that the Seychellois people are "ready for democracy" a strange phrase to use in a country that has officially been a multi-party democracy since 1993 and whose last presidential election, in 2006, was called "credible" by the UN's team of experts, albeit qualified with suggestions of further improvements. The Seychelles came second out of all African countries in the 2010 Imbrahim Index assessing good governance. The public is clearly passionate about politics. However, democracy requires more than political passion and the ability to vote. The most striking characteristic of the lead up to this presidential election is fear.

The current government has been in power since a military coup in the mid-70s overthrew then president, Sir James Mancham. In 1993 a new constitution was written forming the current multi-party system. James Michel is the second president under this system, and the second leader of the SPPF (Seychelles Peoples Progressive Front), now the Parti Lepep succeeding Albert René in 2004.

In 18 years of multi-party democracy there has never been a change of government. This in itself raises questions about the depth of Seychellois democracy. There are more worrying signs: Think Africa Press has seen written evidence of a voter being bribed by the ruling party and of activists for the opposition party being arrested by the police in breach of procedural rules. The state has firm control over the nation's one television station, as well as the main daily newspaper, Nation, which on April 16 featured six pictures of the current president in its first two pages. These various factors seem to contradict even the qualified UN declaration of credibility and the international image of the Seychelles as a beacon of democracy.

The continued success of the ruling party is not in itself an indictment of Seychellois democracy. There is considerable support for the SPPF/Parti Lepep, and good reason for the support as well. The Seychelles boasts free universal healthcare, and if a citizen can not be treated on the islands they are flown to another hospital in another country to be treated, care of the state. There is also a pension system which, while not amounting to complete support (providing 2,200 rupees - about $183 - per month), still provides the poorest a safety net. But there have been a number of presidential elections, and these have all been won by the same party with a reasonably small majority the last was 46% to 54%. It is surprising, therefore, that the results have never gone the way of the opposition party. However, in a small majority political opposition stands out more starkly. It's a small crowd to lose yourself in.

The fear of a watching and knowing state is compounded by individual cases of intimidation and bribery. Think Africa Press has seen evidence that two members of the opposition party, the SNP(Seychelles National Party), were arrested in March for harassment while campaigning. Not only were the activists dealt with by the Officer Commanding the Criminal Investigation Division of the Force, Superintendent Cecile, rather than the local police, as normal procedure would dictate, but the Superintendent also refused to tell the accused who had made the allegations, or any of the specifics of the claim of harassment. Both activists were warned by an intimidating national figure not to do something vague and undefined to unidentified people and then released. This clearly does little to avert fears of a 'big brother' state.

Added to intimidation are allegations of bribery. There are many rumours of bribery, and on both sides. However, Think Africa Press has specific evidence of a letter sent to a construction company with the heading "Presidential Election Campaign Sponsorship", asking the company in question to send a considerable supply of building materials to an individual. It should be noted that building supplies are the usual way, according to hearsay, of bribing would-be supporters.

Allegations of corruption are not limited to James Michel's party. But it seems clear that the party in government has the greatest opportunity to play on the fear of the electorate. Not only is the party in power far richer than the opposition, it also runs a public service system which stretches deep into Seychellois society providing employment to many people. People in these public jobs fear losing their positions or being refused promotion if they vote against the incumbent government.

Moreover, the government has the ability to organise large-scale events functioning as self-promotion tools paid for with public money. An example of this can be seen in the recent Seychelles 2020 EXPO which marketed itself with the following description: "The Seychelles 2020 EXPO has been created to enlighten the Seychellois people, visitors, investors and the world at large on how the present work-in-progress AND planned and visionary activities will benefit them in the years to come. " It is evident from this description that the event was effectively a presentation of James Michel's manifesto for the coming years, lavishly laid on and paid for with national funds.

The influence of the government is also increased by its dominance of the media. The only television channel is run by the state. Although officially SBC is an independent organisation, this is not evident in practice. It does not seem independent, for example, to run an hour-long documentary celebrating the seven years in power of the incumbent leader in the run-up to the presidential elections. There are similar issues with the national radio station. In his 2006 election manifesto Michel promised to "encourage national and private media practitioners to play an active and responsible role in our democracy". However, in the same year legislation was submitted to the National Assembly by Michel's government which made it more difficult for independent organisations to set up radio stations. A peaceful attempt to get a petition against this legislation signed was met by resistance from heavily armed paramilitary police which landed opposition leader, Wavel Ramkalawan, and then-editor of the opposition newspaper Regar, Jean Francois Ferrari, in hospital with head injuries and broken ribs. The government seems intent on maintaining an iron grip on its media dominance.

This media dominance has several effects. The symbolic presence of Michel is huge in comparison to that of Ramkalawan. The six pictures of Michel in the first two pages of the national newspaper, alongside a centrefold spread launching his new book (see above), is typical. There were no pictures, and there was no mention, of Ramkalawan. But beyond the strong media presence of Michel, and the dearth of communication available to the opposition, the dominance of the media also denies the possibility of debate to the electorate a fundamental requirement for democracy. If both points of view are not visible, no effective choice can be made.

This weakening of democracy does not arise from corruption, but is fixed in place by an institutional framework. Similarly there is a lack of transparency in campaign financing because the source of funds need not be declared, and the president can imprison voters thereby preventing them from voting. This law may shortly be ruled unconstitutional in an ongoing case in the Seychelles Constitutional Court, although theconstitution itself is a notoriously difficult document to get hold of.

The people of the Seychelles are passionately political. Until recently there were many demonstrations and rallies testifying to their engagement in political society and their willingness to stand up to those in power, as recorded in Seychelles: the Cry of a People by

Alain St. Ange. Unfortunately the government no longer tolerates such demonstrations because, as one citizen told Think Africa Press, "they would be bad for tourism". Recent peaceful attempts, like the 2006 petition signing and demonstrations against water pollution resulting from the building of President of the UAE, Sheikh Khalifa's new palace, have been met by armed police.

These factors allegations of intimidation, bribery, the apparent omniscience of the government effected by its media dominance compared to a seemingly powerless and invisible opposition, the lack of tolerance for demonstrations and dissent which are met by aggression and violence have a deep impact. Individual instances such as a single arrest, bribery, television show, can be shrugged off and the system as a whole called "credible", as was done by the UN experts. But this is a mistake. It is easy to see that, particularly in a small community, the cumulative effect of all of these various factors make a claim of democratic legitimacy difficult to sustain. For a democracy to function the citizens have to be able to make a free choice when they vote. If they are terrified this freedom is impaired.

Are Seychellois people scared? Well, almost every citizen refused to talk to Think Africa Press once the election was mentioned, although they were open about other aspects of society. Even the Electoral Commissioner, Hendrick Gappy, refused to speak to us. Wavel Ramkalawan, leader of the SNP, told Think Africa Press that "people should not fear politics" a noble sentiment, but one which hinted at the problems which lie behind his earlier statement, "the Seychelles is ready for democracy". The citizens may be ready, but James Michel is not.

International Corruption in Africa, The Strange Case of [Seychelles] and South Africa.

The Topic OF Corruption has emerged at the top of the agenda in recent dealings between African governments and the Western donors on whom many are heavily dependant. It is notoriously difficult to define corruption, 1 but it is generally understood to entail the use of an official position for purposes of private enrichment or illegitimate advantage. During the 1970s and 1980s, there was a stream of books on corruption in Africa or on closely related concepts such as neo-patrimonialism, prebendalism and kleptocracy. Particularly since a World Bank report in 1989 explicitly spoke of a 'crisis of governance' in Africa soth of the Sahara,much of the discussion of corruption south of the Sahara has been subsumed in a wider debate on governance.

The literature on corruption or on governance in Africa more generally tends to adopt a national perspective, investigating how national elites use corruption or manipulation of public policy to enrich themselves and maintain themselves in power. It is rather less frequent, at least in the academic literature, to encounter detailed studies of the relationship between corruption in various parts of Africa and that in industrialized countries. The present article is an attempt to trace the development of corruption in one part of Africa in a global context. It demonstrates how the ease with which capital can be transferred and commodities bought and sold and the speed of modern communication in general have been given considerable impetus to the linking of corrupt practices across borders, and that this process of trans-national corruption was considerably encouraged by the Cold War. The main focus of study is Seychelles, a small country but one which has the merit-if that is the right word-of providing interesting data on the subject under discussion. After independence in 1976 Seychelles was subject to intense international diplomatic and military activity, often of a covert nature, due largely to the islands' strategic location, which made them an asset both in US-Soviet rivalry in the Indian Ocean and in the more localized patterns of conflict stemming from South Africa's drive to assert its hegemony in southern Africa, notably by destabilizing or manipulating neighbouring states. This led to attempts to subvert or influence the islands' government by bribery and by force, while more powerful governments and business interests associated with political parties as far afield as Italy manipulated Seychelles' status as a sovereign state in order to perform various transactions of dubious legality. There is some evidence also that the islands were used for financial transactions by arms-dealers and as a staging-post for drug trafficking. These various interests became intertwined with each other and with the Seychelles' government's own policies, having a demonstrable effect on governance in the islands.

It should be emphasized at the outset that not all the transactions, individuals or circumstances described here can be described as corrupt. On the contrary, one of the principal conclusions which can be drawn from the present essay is that grand corruption, sometimes masquer ading as raison d'Etat, shapes the environment in which individual politicians, diplomats and business people are obliged to operate.

Seychelles

The Republic of Seychelles consists of over a hundred islands scattered over a wide area of the western Indian Ocean. Most of its population-a mere 60,000 people at independence in 1976, and less than 100,000 today-is concentrated on just two islands. For a century and a half Seychelles was a remote and insignificant part of the British Empire. Only in 1971, as Britain renounced its colonial presence in the Indian Ocean, did the British government endow the islands with an international airport which was to transform their economic and strategic position by providing easy physical access to the rest of the world.

Britain's strategy for decolonization in the western Indian Ocean from the 1960s entailed divesting itself of colonies while detaching from the colonial administrative territories strategically useful islands which could become the sites for air and naval bases politically easier to manage than bases in more populous territories. As Seychelles became independent, Britain at first attempted to retain its influence by supplying the country's first president, Sir James Mancham, with covert political finance and security assistance. But Britain's political role in the region rapidly declined as Britain lost its ability to project its power world-wide. As the Indian Ocean emerged as a major site of Cold War strategic interest, it was the United States which tended to take over former British assets in the area. The US government built its principal air and naval base in the Indian Ocean a thousand miles to the east of Seychelles, on the island of Diego Garcia, a former dependency of Mauritius whose entire population the British government deported before leasing the island to the US. As part of its global military communications network the US government also built in the Seychelles an important satellite tracking station.

President Mancham was staunchly pro-Western in his foreign policy and seems to have envisaged attracting Middle Eastern petro-dollars for the economic development of his country, most notably through his highly public friendship with the Saudi businessman and arms dealer Adnan Kashoggi. But within one year of his election, on the night of 4-5 June 1977, President Mancham was overthrown in a coup by his prime minister, France Albert Rene. Rene's coup was aided by the government of Tanzania, and the new president soon took Seychelles into the left-wing camp in African politics. It became a one-party state. Nevertheless Rene continued his predecessor's policy of encouraging the creation of a tourist industry in the islands, and this has helped to make the country today an economic success by African standards. President Rene, realis ing that Western holiday-makers were Seychelles' most obvious customers and source of foreign exchange, strove to maintain correct relations with Western governments as well as with the socialist countries where his personal political sympathies lay.

Much of the world's oil cargoes pass through the Indian Ocean, and in a period of turbulence in the Middle East and of Soviet ambitions to create a naval presence in the Indian Ocean, and especially after the 1979 revolution in Iran and the Soviet invasion of Afghanistan, the whole of the western Indian ocean rapidly increased in strategic importance. Seychelles was sufficiently irnponant in Cold War strategic planning for the US government to be concerned by the pro-Soviet sympathies of the islands' government after the 1977 coup. France too had strategic ambitions in the Indian Ocean which caused it to take an interest in the islands; the government of Seychelles seems to have suspected the French government of being connected with a coup plot uncovered in the islands in 1979, expelling French military advisors and replacing them with Tanzanians and Algerians. The Soviet Union maintained a large embassy staff in Seychelles and for several years the Soviet ambassador was Mikhail Orlov, regarded by Western intelligence agencies as a senior KGB officer, said to have previously worked as the chief of the important KGB station in Turkey. Soviet warships paid counesy calls to the 'islands and the Soviet Union also proffered other forms of assistance. Moreover by the early 1980s there were more than 100 North Korean military advisors in the islands. Another country interested in Seychelles was South Africa, whose government was concerned to prevent the Soviet Union from extending its influence in southern Africa, and which saw the Republic of Seychelles as a potential asset in South Africa's own ambition of securing regional hegemony.

Within a shon time of its independence in 1976, then, Seychelles had become of considerable strategic interest to the two super-powers and to a number of lesser powers-France, South Afyica and others-all of which sought to exercise influence in the islands. The country was exceptionally vulnerable to the pressures which larger governments could exert, largely because of its small size and tiny army, and perhaps also because its tourist industry was reliant on Seychelles' being able to maintain an image of tranquillity and unspoiled beauty in order to attract holiday-makers. One might add that the manner in which President Rene took power in 1977 was a significant cause of instability, for, like most other coups, it had established a precedent for the transfer of power by unconstitutional means which was to put into question the government's legitimacy in years to come.

Beset by the attention of foreign secret services and by plots from within, President Rene turned for help to a friend, Giovanni Mario Ricci, an Italian businessman who had been living in Seychelles since shortly before independence. Due to the influence he had with Rene, Ricci was to become an important intermediary for foreigners wishing to cultivate commercial or political relations in Seychelles, as we will shortly describe in more detail. Mario Ricci was born near Lucca, Italy, in 1929. Convicted of fraud in Italy in 1958, he had gone to seek his fortune abroad. He was convicted a second time, in Switzerland, this time for possessing counterfeit currency. Ricci lived Mexico and Haiti before making his way to Somalia where he set up a business exporting grapefruit. He was expelled from Somalia for reasons unknown around 1974, moving to settle in Seychelles. He was a distinctive figure in the islands, instantly recognizable by his long beard, grown white since he first went to live in Seychelles.

Ricci became President Rene's friend and unofficial financial advisor. In 1978 he set up a company, the Seychelles Trust Company, in a joint venture with the Seychelles government. The government granted to the Seychelles Trust Company sole rights to incorporate off-shore companies and to act as resident agent for foreign companies and foundations registered in Seychelles, which could operate free of tax. The granting of this right to a private company was unique in that it made the Seychelles Trust Company the only private offshore business registration company in the world, and, in effect, Seychelles became the world's first socialist tax haven. In 1981 the government sold its shares in the Seychelles Trust Company, leaving Ricci in sole control. The cost of registering a foreign company, payable to the government, was a mere

·1,SOO rupees, or 8300. It was to Ricci that President Rene turned for help after an attempted coup in 1981 (which is discussed in more detail below) had convinced him of the need to improve his government's security. At the President's request, Ricci hired private detectives to keep the exiled opposition under surveillance. In 1982 a private detective employed by Ricci succeeded in planting a recording device in a London hotel room being used by Seychellois exiles to plot a coup against the government, and the tape was handed to the British press. Both the single party and the government of Seychelles came to rely on Ricci for various financial services, and accepted cash from him, in President Rene's words 'when [the government] needed to finance something for which we didn't immediately have the money'. Ricci in tum received privileged treatment from the government, and when one of his companies was nationalized, he was paid in cash, whereas other companies in a similar position received only government bonds. President Rene later stated that he had taken the precaution of asking the Italian authorities whether Ricci had a criminal record, but 'they told us that they had nothing on him. '2Ricci was associated with some distinctly unusual companies in addition to the Seychelles Trust Company. In 1982 he was listed as a director of an entity immodestly entitled International Monetary Funding, or IMF, for short, not be confused with the International Monetary Fund. In 1984 he was accredited to Seychelles as a diplomat representing the Sovereign Order of the Coptic Catholic Knights of Malta which, it emerged, was a commercial company incorporated in New York. Seychelles was the only state in the world to recognize the order. President Rene later claimed that his government had granted Ricci diplomatic status in the mistaken belief that Ricci's Knights of Malta was in fact the Sovereign Order of Saint John, Knights of Malta, the well-known Vatican order of chivalry. Through his accreditation Ricci gained the right to use a diplomatic pouch and a diplomatic passport, and eventually he was to become the doyen of the diplomatic corps in the islands. President Rene also confided diplomatic missions to him, such as the improvement of relations with Somalia, where Ricci had once lived and where he still had useful contacts. Ricci increasingly used one of his many companies, GMR (named after his own initials), as a flagship for various interests. According to GMR's own company brochure it was 'a conglomerate of companies which operates throughout the world' and was 'managed from the operational headquarters in the Republic of Seychelles'. At various times GMR's management, consisting mostly of Ricci and members of his and his wife's families, claimed to control companies in as many as 24 countries, including several in southern and eastern Africa as well as in more conventional business locations such as Britain and Switzerland, and tax havens including Panama, Liechtenstein and Luxembourg. This and Ricci's other companies in the islands were registered and run in conform ity with Seychelles law. Already by the early 1980s, Ricci had acquired a reputation as someone who could be approached by anyone who wished to transact some form of business in Seychelles. Although having no official government position, he was diplomat, unofficial head of security, businessman and financial advisor to President Rene all rolled into one.

South Africa

Among the countries which had developed an interest in Seychelles was South Africa. At the time of the islands' independence in 1976, South Africa's National Party government was already feeling the impact of diplomatic isolation and of the gradual development of a military threat to its security. The government in Pretoria placed increasing importance on securing influence and the capacity to exercise force both within and outside its borders by clandestine means, notably through the development of its secret services (especially the Bureau of State Security, established in 1969) and the Department of Information. For as long as Namibia remained a South African colony, and Rhodesia, Mozambique and Angola remained under colonial or settler rule, South Africa itself was insulated from external aggression, but the situation changed rapidly with the independence of Angola and

Mozambique in 1975 and the Soweto uprising of 1976.

The Department of Information was an agency of the South African government whose tasks included the covert distribution of government monies-in other words, bribery-to buy influence at home and abroad. This included in Seychelles. During Sir James Mancham's brief tenure of the presidency Seychelles was regularly visited by South African secret servants carrying '[bags full] of. bribe money to secure South African interests', the editor of the Johannesburg Sunday Express later recalled. In 1978 the Department of Information's role was exposed in a political scandal known as 'Muldergate' or 'Infogate', in which it was revealed that the Department had not only bribed journalists and secretly bought newspapers at home and abroad in a bid to secure better public relations, but that senior civil servants and politicians in South Africa had abused the Department's lack of parliamentary accountability for purposes of personal enrichment-in other words, corruption. The Muldergate scandal became closely associated with the struggle to succeed the ailing Prime Minister, John Vorster, and to supplant the influence wielded by the Bureau of State Security (BOSS), which was headed by a political appointee, the prime minister's friend and confidant General H. J. van den Bergh. The favourite to succeed Vorster, Dr Connie Mulder, was disgraced as a result of the scandal and lost his claim to the premiership.

The person who emerged victorious from the political in-fighting surrounding the Muldergate scandal to become prime minister of South Africa in 1978 was the Defence Minister, P. W. Botha, who had powerful support from the generals of the South African Defence Force (SADF). The military men resented van den Bergh's and BOSS's pre-eminence in security manners and believed that the changed situation in southern Africa necessitated a complete overhaul of security policy under military direction. The security chiefs, the 'securocrats' as they came to be known, were to acquire great power under P. W. Botha's premiership and later presidency. They unveiled a comprehensive new strategy whose centre piece was the defence of the South African state in the face of what the government saw as a comprehensive threat, a 'total onslaught' in Prime Minister Botha's words, orchestrated by the Soviet Union. Seychelles had a minor but distinct role in this strategy. The islands offered not only potential military facilities but also possible use as a base for clandestine trading purposes in the face of economic sanctions, especially after the Iranian revolution of 1979 had threatened South Africa's main supply of oil. South Africa in fact was to acquire most of its oil after 1979 from Saudi Arabia and the Gulf states. Due to a combination of the new defence strategy in Pretoria and the change in government in Seychelles in 1977, the South African secret services decided that bribery was no longer the most effective means of acquiring influence in the islands. In 1978 Seychellois exiles in South Africa, acting on behalf of ex-President Mancham, began discussions with officials concerning a coup attempt to be launched in Seychelles. The BOSS case officer who became most closely concerned with this scheme was one Martin Dolinchek. As plans for the Seychelles' coup developed the SADF lobbied to acquire control of the project, and the operation became the subject of an intense bureaucratic struggle between the military and the civilian intelligence service, The National Intelligence Service (NIS). The NIS was the direct descendant of the former BOSS, which had been disgraced in the Muldergate scandal and subsequently over hauled and twice renamed. Prime Minister Botha was more sympathetic to the military men than he was to the civilian intelligence service. In the end the government allocated planning for the Seychelles' coup operation to Military Intelligence, while the protests of the civilian intelligence service were mollified by the appointment of Martin Dolinchek as a liaison officer on behalf of the NIS. 35 In order to provide a screen of deniability to the Seychelles' coup attempt the operation was entrusted to Mike Hoare, an Irish mercenary soldier who had made his name in the Congo but was now living in South Africa as a civilian. Hoare was later to testify that the coup plans were approved by the South African Cabinet and that weapons were provided by South African Military Intelligence. 36 Most of the 45 or so people selected to carry out the coup were members of South African special forces, several of them former Rhodesian soldiers, some with earlier. experience in the British army.

On 25 November 1981 Hoare and his men landed at Seychelles international airport disguised as tourists, members of a drinking-club called the Ancient Order of Frothblowers. After a customs officer had found weapons in the luggage of one of the purported tourists, the invaders fought a brief gun-battle at the airport and escaped aboard an Air India jet which happened to be on the tarmac and which they hijacked. They left behind five soldiers, a female accomplice and also Dolinchek, the intelligence man. The Seychelles' government arrested and tried the six men, acquiring from them full information on the planning of the coup. Four of the six were sentenced to death. Hoare and some others were tried on their return to South Africa.

The Pretoria government, severely embarrassed, opened negotiations for the return of the six convicted mercenaries, and they were eventually returned to South Africa in rnid-1983. The conditions for their release were not publicized, and only gradually did it become apparent that in the course of negotiations the South African government had not only paid to President Rene a ransom of S3 million, 39 but that this was part of a broader

understanding with President Rene personally. His cabinet was not informed of the progress of the talks nor of the ransom payment. President Rene, alarmed by the succession of coup attempts against him, asked Mario Ricci to help improve his security service. He realized that in order to survive he needed to adjust his foreign policy to accommodate South African interests, at least in some measure. The government also took a series of steps designed to mend fences with both South Africa and the US, whose own Centritl Intelligence Agency (CIA) had had foreknowl edge of the coup attempt,and there was a notable shift in Seychelles' voting record in the United Nations and other international fora. The advent of a Socialist government in France in 1981 also helped to ease the pressure on the islands' government, since France maintained an interest in the region notably through its possession of the island of Reunion and military base in Djibouti. For its part, in 1983 the South African government uncovered a further coup plan which was under discussion and expelled from its territory Seychellois opposition activists including Gerard Hoarau, a former seminary student who had been detained in Seychelles in connection with the 1979 coup plot and had gone into exile. Hoarau was a cousin of Rene's wife and, speaking fluent Italian, had previously been a friend of Ricci.

It appears to have been in the aftermath of the 1981 coup attempt, during negotiations for the release of the six South African mercenaries, that the South African secret services first came fully to appreciate Ricci's significance as a potential intermediary with President Rene. At that time the number two person in section A, the foreign desk of the South African Security Police, was Craig Williamson, the country's best-known spy. Recruited by the Security Police while he was still at university in South Africa, Williamson had posed as a left-wing student activist and gone into exile, where he succeeded in infiltrating the ANC. In 1979 his true allegiance was revealed and he returned to Pretoria to take up a post at Security Police headquarters. To compound the damage inflicted on the ANC, he absconded from the organization with substantial funds in his possession. These he had turned over to the Security Police, and the ANC's money was later used to buy a farm near Pretoria which was to become a base for operations by Security Police death-squads. In 1985 Williamson resigned from the Security Police and publicly announced that he was going into business. It was not announced that he had at the same time been commissioned as a colonel in South African Military Intelligence. Williamson later explained his resignation from the Security

Police on the grounds that 'I decided to get involved in proper intelligence work, especially on the international scene'. By the mid-1980s Williamson and Ricci had developed a close relationship. In 1986, the year after Williamson's resignation from the police, Ricci's GMR company was registered to do business in South Africa and

Williamson was appointed managing director of GMR South Africa and vice-president of GMR world-wide. In GMR's own company litera ture, the GMR conglomerate was henceforth said to be 'controlled from the executive offices based in Switzerland and South Africa. ' The company prospectus represented GMR as a holding company which owned various companies world-wide. Some GMR subsidiary companies, it said, were local acquisitions made in the hope of being able to resell them again at a profit. Other subsidiaries it described as 'parked', dormant companies which could be activated to deal with specific transactions if necessary. Williamson assisted Ricci in acquiring permanent resident's status in South Africa. 47 He scoffed at pointed questions from journalists about Ricci's mysterious background, suggesting that any debatable points in Ricci's curriculum vitae could be explained quite easily. 'There is no hot money, or mafia money, in the GMR operation,' Williamson declared to the press. There is no evidence that Ricci was aware of Williamson's commission in Military Intelligence, but he must certainly have known of his earlier career in the Security Police.

The opening of GMR in South Africa, and the appointment of Craig Williamson as its managing director, gave Ricci access to business oppor tunities in South Africa, and by the same token it gave Williamson access to the GMR empire and to Ricci's business connections. Williamson hinted to journalists that his purpose was to use Seychelles and the GMR company to avoid the trade sanctions which were being applied with increasing severity to South Africa. 'I would like to assist South Africa in the economic warfare facing it', Williamson was quoted as saying, when asked about his new career as the chief executive of Ricci's GMR company. Williamson described GMR as 'flexible' and talked about how it could be used as a front by other companies seeking to do business with South Africa. 'If [GMR] is faced with anti-sanctions laws,' he said, 'it will restructure its activities to avoid any inhibiting laws. 'On another occasion Williamson divulged: 'we are involved in trade in strategic commodities. I don't want to go into details, but GMR has a background in oil. 'In effect, although Ricci himself had virtually no experience in the oil business, he had earlier helped to introduce to Seychelles some Italians with extensive expertise in the oil business, to whom Williamson may have been referring. This will be discussed further below.

Williamson, cultivating his new persona as a trader, gave seminars to South African businessmen looking for new markets in the Far East and lectured on how to evade sanctions. He seemed intent on creating a political niche for himself as well, and his political ambitions clearly had support from the very top of the ruling party. In 1987 he stood for parliament as a candidate for the National Party in a suburb of Johannesburg but failed to secure election. Not to be thwarted, President Botha appointed Williamson a member of the President's Council.

By this time, South Africa's relationship with Seychelles was thoroughly ambiguous. Seychelles was often represented in the South African press, and the Western press generally, as pro-Soviet and anti-apartheid. In reality, Pretoria had developed closer relations with the government in Victoria in the months after the 1981 mercenary coup attempt and had expelled Seychellois opposition leaders from South Africa, but the South African secret services at the same time conspired with a group of coup-plotters based in Britain through a diplomat at the South African Embassy in London. The South African secret services eventually betrayed the coup plot to the Seychelles government in August 1986 and in effect aborted the plan. It seems that the South African strategy was to cultivate all sides in Seychelles with a view to cementing its own influence. After the August 1986 coup plot, South Africa's Military Intelligence had the Seychelles government under effective control, largely through Williamson and the relationship he had established with Ricci. GMR South Africa shared its Johannesburg office with another company controlled by Williamson, named Longreach, which acquired responsibility for government security in Seychelles after 1986. Years later, after the African National Congress had come to power, Williamson was to admit that Longreach was in fact secretly owned by Military

Intelligence. Seychelles was all the more useful as a Military Intelligence asset because of its government's pro-Soviet reputation. In matters of strategic deception, the South African secret services had made considerable advances since the ham-fisted bribery of the Department of Information and the 1981 mercenary fiasco.

Although Longreach purponed to deal mainly in risk analysis, claiming officially to be advising businessmen on conditions for investment in southern Africa, particularly in Mozambique, Uganda and Burundi,it in fact operated as an agent of Military Intelligence both inside and outside South Africa. Williamson once admitted that the company had engaged a French mercenary to carry out the attempted murder of President Lennox Sebe of Ciskei. This, it transpired, was part of an operation by South African Military Intelligence aimed at incorporating Ciskei into a larger new homeland. South Africa's transition to democracy after 1990 did not mean the end of the covert networks established in earlier years, including those in Seychelles. Senior South African ministers continued to visit Seychelles: in April

1991 Defence Minister Magnus Malan visited the islands, follow ing Foreign Minister Pik Botha who had also been on a visit earlier in the year. 57 In 1994, the press reported that a South African naval officer, Commodore Willem 'Ters' Ehlers, who had succeeded Williamson as chief executive of GMR in South Africa, had negotiated with the Za1rean government the purchase of some S40 million of arms. These weapons were almost certainly intended for eventual transfer to Rwanda. Ehlers had worked as a private secretary to President P. W. Botha and it was in this capacity that he had first met Mario Ricci. After Botha's retirement, Ehlers had gone to work for GMR, apparently from 1990 until around 1992. A spokesman for GMR said in 1994 that both Williamson and Ehlers had ceased to work for the company. 59 Williamson had indeed resigned on 31 December 1988 and Ricci in November 1991. A lead ing US human rights organization, Human Rights Watch, repeated the allegations the following year.

This was one of several cases in the 1990s indicating the extent to which the South African state arms company ARMSCOR remained a major inter national arms dealer even after the end of the armed struggle for control of South Africa, both selling arms manufactured in South Africa and brokering third-party deals. In Africa today arms-dealing is a lucrative business, and also one with obvious political implications. Even since the demise of the National Party government in 1994 ARMSCOR continues to be something of a law unto itself, still largely staffed by the personnel of the apartheid era carrying out secretive weapons deals, some of which have embarrassed the ANC government, and making use of commercial networks created in earlier years in both public and private sectors. As with all modem weapons-deals, ARMSCOR's commercial sales have political implications. This is true of every country with a weapons-exporting industry. In the case of South Africa, however, the question is to know to what extent arms sales are under effective government control.

Covert operations and corruption

GMR and Longreach were only two of the hundreds of companies set up or acquired by the South African security establishment in pursuit of the strategy of counter-revolution. Some of these companies were used to trade in products subject to international sanctions, including oil, but also in less legitimate products such as ivory and rhino horn. One of Longreach's original board of directors, James Anthony White, a former member of the Rhodesian Selous Scouts, was reported to have an interest in the ivory trade. Front companies were used to channel weapons or supplies to South African allies in Angola, Mozambique and elsewhere. Some, like the network run by the main SADF death-squad, the Civil Co-operation Bureau, were used to carry out assassinations, and others for money-laundering or for peddling political influence.

Another Military Intelligence front with which Williamson was associated, the International Freedom Foundation, succeeded in enlisting senior memben; of the Republican Party in the US, including Senator Jesse Helms, later to become chairman of the Senate Foreign Affairs Committee, in the campaign to defend apartheid. The securing of influence in Seychelles was very useful for various activities of this type. Thus, Chieftain Airlines, a front company used by the South African secret services which was later investigated for corrup tion, applied to the South African National Transportation Commission to By Boeing 737s between Johannesburg, the Comoros and Seychelles. The Comoros too were used by South Africa for clandestine arms shipments to the Middle East, and from 1979 South Africa paid the French mercenaries who were to run the islands' Presidential Guard until 1990. Pretoria's 'total strategy' required massive resources to implement and it required the people who managed it, the securocrats, to become interested in spheres of activity which are traditionally outside the scope of the military. Some of this was done openly; some of it required deception, either in the form of secret operations, or the establishment of secret organs of government, or the use of covert activity, meaning actions whose real purpose is other than the apparent one. The total strategy implied centralization of power and decision-making and a great expansion both of the role of the state and of the military and security branches within it. This had obvious political and constitutional implications for South Africa, and the increasing use of covert or clandes tine operations in the service of the total strategy also had implications for the accountability of government and, hence, its tendency towards corruption.

Any sort of covert operation has numerous ramifications. If a military unit is secretly to channel arms to an ally, such as was actually done by the SADF in Angola and Mozambique, it must first procure the necessary weapons and ammunition. That means either manufacturing, capturing or purchasing them. Since the supply of these weapons is to be secret, the first option is not be recommended, as the weapons must not be traceable to the actual supplier ifthey fall into the wrong hands. It was far better for the SADF to capture Soviet-supplied weapons in Angola and then supply them to RENAMO in Mozambique, or even to buy them from Warsaw Pact countries on behalf of their clients, than to supply RENAMO and UNITA with standard SADF equipment.

Whatever the source of the weapons, a covert armourer must establish a safe channel for their delivery, probably requiring aircraft and pilots, possibly ships, or at least trucks and drivers. Again, in the interests of secrecy, it is best not to use aircraft of the regular air force or army vehicles for this purpose, since that would make the operation too easY. to trace back to the supplier government. Far better to use a front company, an airline or transport company which, like Chieftain Airlines or like the Frama company in Namibia, is apparently in the private sector, but is in reality controlled by the secret services. Pilots and truck-drivers are often men with families, and they require salaries, insurance and pensions, which must also be arranged discreetly since the operatives are not officially on the government payroll but on that of a front company.

All of this means extra work for civil servants who must be employed for the purpose. It also requires money, which, to preserve confidentiality, can come from the secret budget of the state or from other sources. The latter are preferable since private-sector funding is less easy for hostile politicians, journalists and others to trace back to the government. The latter, in fact, is precisely what happened in the Muldergate affair, in that the funds used were relatively easy to trace and implicated politicians in decisions which they later found it impossible to deny with any degree of plausibility. Sometimes it is possible to 'launder' state funds destined for a clandestine operation so as to make them appear as if they emanate from the private business sector, or perhaps genuine businessmen can be induced to finance projects which are primarily of strategic interest. Again, these were all features of the financing of the Muldergate operation in the 1970s.

Some front companies may actually generate commercial profits, which can be either diverted or ploughed back into the operation. If money is to be generated from clandestine trade or illicit business, it must be laundered or cleared through the banking system in such a way as to disguise its origin and destination, and this may involve breaking the banking laws, possibly of several countries. A pliable bank, or even a bank secretly controlled by the secret services, is an asset. Hence

Chieftain Airlines was associated with a bank established in the Ciskei homeland which took unlicensed deposits and engaged in currency fraud.

The bank's owner, a friend of Cabinet ministers Magnus Malan and Pik Botha, was in business with one Vito Palazzolo, an Italian who had worked as a money-launderer in the US and Europe for the important 'Pizza connection' mafia syndicate and had subsequently settled in South Africa. The difficulties inherent in money-laundering, it is relevant to note, are only one of several problems which secret servants intent on under taking covert or clandestine operations share with drug-traffickers and other professional criminals. The creation of secret or covert networks, maintained with secret funds, inevitably attracts the attention of pro fessional criminals and tempts otherwise honest people to steal, since the funds involved are publicly unaccountable. So it was in South Africa. Some companies set up by the secret services took illegal com missions or 'kickbacks' on otherwise legitimate contracts awarded by the government. This was particularly common in the South African home lands or bantustans, where there was little effective legal supervision of public works contracts and where corruption was rife. Other branches of the South African government used intermediaries to import oil, since South Africa's international isolation sometimes meant that a middleman had to be employed to disguise a transaction.

This cost money in the form of the agent's commission and offered opportunities for official corruption. Front companies are commonly used by secret services operating in pursuit of state interests, and familiarity with their functioning is clearly part of the tradecraft of intelligence officers and specialists in low-intensity conflict. Politicians are necessary to any such operation, since their authority is needed to legitimize any covert operation, and in fact the element of political athority in such circumstances is crucial since it is political responsibility alone which constitutes the dividing line between a state-sponsored covert or clandestine operation and a purely criminal affair, carried out for private interest by professional criminals or by secret servants who have crossed the line to become rogue elements, disowned by politicians and liable to criminal prosecution. If a dishonest politician, whose authority is needed to provide top cover for an operation, demands a percentage of the financial transactions taking place within his or her sphere of interest, their demands can hardly be resisted. This was clearly the case in South Africa, as Dr Eschel Rhoodie, a senior official responsible for covert funding in the 1970s, has testified.

The recent history of South Africa shows clearly how the pursuit of state interests by covert or clandestine means, and the provision of funds or the implementation of plans which are not publicly accountable, encouraged the growth of corruption in South Africa and elsewhere. The system developed into a complex set of relationships in which secret services directly or indirectly developed commercial interests, and made increasing use of violence as well. In effect the secret services became associated with a spectrum of commercial and military or political activity. At one extreme were ventures such as the 1981 mercenary attack on Seychelles which were entirely military in nature. At the other end of the spectrum were legitimate commercial companies such as GMR. All of these had in common the presence of the South African secret services and, in particu lar, Military Intelligence. From the relatively straightforward bribery of the Department of Information there was a direct line of progression to the complex of commercial relationships in airlines, companies and legitimate or illegitimate trade in ivory and, according to at least one authoritative source, drugs. It was only after it had suffered severe embarrassment from the attempt to take over the government of Seychelles in 1981 that the South African secret services settled on subtler means. It was in this way, as the South Africans looked for ways of securing influence with President Rene's government, that they crune to appreciate the advantages offered by Mario Ricci's position in the islands and his contacts elsewhere.

Political finance and corruption

Others too were interested by Ricci's position in Seychelles. In 1980, a friend of Ricci's, the Roman banker Roberto Memmo, learned of Ricci's rights to incorporate offshore companies in the islands and established an offshore bank there, Roberto Memmo Investment Banking. Although it was not publicly known at that time, Memmo was a member of the Italian masonic lodge P-2, a secret organization of leading figures in Italian business, the security and intelligence services and politics, which, when its existence was revealed, caused a sensation in Italy. A parliamentary commission of inquiry in Italy established that the lodge had been closely connected with right-wing politics. In effect, during the 1970s P-2 and the Italian secret services had conspired in a strategy aimed at preventing the election of a communist government in Italy, including by inspiring acts of right-wing terror such as the 1980 bombing of Bologna railway station. Leading members of P-2 had also succeeded in infiltrating the finances of the Vatican. The full extent of corruption in Italian public. life was to be fully laid bare only by the mani pulite ('Operation Clean Hands') investigations of the 1990s.

At the heart of politics in Italy for several decades, it has now been proven, was a system whereby the main political parties received kickbacks in return for the awarding of public contracts from businesses and particularly from Italian parastatal companies over which politicians were able to exert influence. Secret networks like P-2 enabled obscure figures, such as the Venerable Master of the P-2 lodge Licio Gelli, to influence or even to blackmail politicians and government officials and also to negotiate with other important elements in Italian life, including the mafia and the Vatican. The illicit payments negotiated through such networks between businessmen and politicians were illegally transferred to the bank accounts of various operators of the system and of individual politicians, usually through an elaborate series of transactions involving paper com panies established for the purpose, and often by using offshore facilities in Switzerland, the Caribbean and elsewhere. The amounts of money involved were huge. One of the parastatal companies most deeply involved in this process was the Italian state oil company, the Ente Nazionale Idrocarburi

(ENI), which was eventually found, as a result of the mani pulite judicial investigations, to have channelled over a billion and a half dollars to Italian political parties in illegal payments. As part of the political spoils system, Italy's leading political parties had also divided along geographical lines the political oversight of the large Italian develop ment budget, with the Italian Socialist Party taking Somalia, for example, and another party, Mozambique. Each party thus took its cut of kick backs from contracts given to Italian companies, as did the relevant officials and politicians in Africa itself. This system of political financing produced regular scandals in Italy whenever elements of the country's clandestine system of power-broking were made public. It was only in the early 1990s that circumstances permitted Italian judges to move against the political parties and influence-peddlers.

Among the most prominent scandals produced by this system was the 1982 collapse of the Banco Ambrosiano with unrecoverable loans of some Sl. 3 billion, at that time one of the largest bank collapses in history, and the mysterious death of the Bank's chairman, Roberto Calvi, found hanging beneath London's Blackfriars Bridge. The bad loans had been made to shell companies actually controlled by Calvi and by the Vatican bank, the Institute of Religious Works. A considerable amount of the money, perhaps $250 million, had been siphoned off by the Venerable Master of the P-2 masonic lodge. The Institute of Religious Works lost some SSOO million of Vatican money through its transactions with Banco Ambrosiano. A number of people closely associated with the Banco Ambrosiano, with ENI, and with the illicit provision of public funds to Italian political parties had dealings in Seychelles in the 1980s. Roberto Memmo, for example, worked as a commercial agent for ENI. A significant figure in Italy's political and financial underworld, f<rancesco Pazienza, arrived in Seychelles, on the run from the Italian police, in 1983. Pazienza was well-known in Italy, and his name had already been associated with several major scandals. Pazienza had been a protege of a chief of Italian military intelligence, General Giuseppe Santovito, who fell into disgrace when his membership of the P-2 masonic lodge

became known, and Pazienza had been employed a·s a personal assistant by Roberto Calvi at a time when the Banco Ambrosiano chairman was desperately seeking financial support from the secret networks of Italian finance to cover the huge hole in his accounts. It was Pazienza who was in fact the originator of the Sovereign Order of the Coptic Catholic Knights of Malta, the company which Ricci was to represent as a diplomat in Seychelles, and it was from him that Ricci acquired the company.

Pazienza's extraordinary range of contacts in the fields of business, politics and intelligence extended to the US, where he had at one stage worked with a number of Americans associated with Ronald Reagan's 1980 election campaign. While Pazienza was an inveterate liar and fabricator of tall stories, it does appear that ·he had helped the Reagan campaign by supplying intelligence material calculated to embarrass Reagan's opponent, the incumbent President Jimmy Carter. When he arrived in Seychelles in 1983, Pazienza was wanted for questioning by the Italian police in connection with various affairs includ ing the collapse of the Banco Ambrosiano. His ambitions were dazzling.

He met Ricci and members of the government and shared with them his ideas for turning Seychelles into an entrepot and operations centre for commodity transactions of various kinds, using the off-shore rights held by Ricci. He claimed to have the support of leading financiers in the US and elsewhere, and indeed many of those he named did not deny knowing Pazienza. Among the schemes which Pazienza claims to have conceived were plans to sell fishing-rights to Mexican interests and to use the islands as a base for dealing in cut-price Mexican oil. In November 1984 Pazienza learned from a government minister that two Italian policemen were on their way to Seychelles to arrest him and he hastily left the islands, travelling on a genuine Seychellois diplomatic passport. He was later arrested in the US and extradited to Italy. Following Memmo and Pazienza to Seychelles came another Italian connected to both ENI and the Banco Ambrosiano, the financier Florio Fiorini. ss Fiorini was the former finance director of ENI who had resigned after he was revealed to have prepared without proper authoriz ation a scheme to use ENI funds in a bid to save the Banco Ambrosiano, shortly before the Bank's collapse.

During his career at ENI Fiorini had become a leading figure in the jungle of Italian political finance and had demonstrated a remarkable talent for financial manipulation. After leaving ENI he had gone on to build up a business empire on his own behalf. His main vehicle was a company called Societe anonyme suisse d'exportations agricoles, known as SASEA. 90 SASEA was an obscure Swiss agricultural products' company, part-owned by the Vatican, which had little to recommend it other than a listing on the Geneva stock exchange. Shortly after the collapse of the Banco Ambrosiano and his own departure from ENI, Fiorini assembled a consortium of businessmen, many of them previously associated with both ENI and the Banco Ambrosiano, who acquired and recapitalized SASEA.

The company's chairman was no less than Nello Celio, a former president of Switzerland. In effect,

Fiorini and his colleagues transformed SASEA into a merchant bank, buying, asset-stripping and selling companies and financing acquisitions in Europe and North America, while continuing to work closely with Italian politicians. Fiorini had especially close contacts with leaders of the Italian Socialist Party, especially Prime Minister Bettino Craxi and Foreign Minister Gianni De Michaelis, both of whom were to be convicted of corruption in 1995. (Their conviction is currently pending an appeal).

Fiorini visited Seychelles for the first time in 1983 or 1984 and met both Mario Ricci and President Rene. Fiorini had the idea of acquiring an oil-trading facility in Seychelles, and he and SASEA worked with President Rene to nationalize the Shell oil company in the islands. In 1985 the government nationalized Shell and replaced it with the Seychelles National Oil Company (SNOC), which also took a share-holding in a number of SNOC subsidiary companies. An Italian oil firm, a shareholder in SASEA with close associations with ENI, obtained a contract to manage the Seychelles' government's new oil interests. The government and Fiorini explained the nationalization by saying that it would enable Seychelles to sell fuel to aircraft and ships visiting the islands. Pazienza, by this time in detention, alleged that it was in fact the realization of his idea of using the islands to trade oil on the world market.

It was probably this development of Italian-run oil interests in Seychelles which prompted the South African Military Intelligence officer, Craig Williamson, to suggest in 1986 that he was joining GMR because of what he called its 'background in oil'. After Williamson's entry into GMR, there were rumours that the government of Seychelles and its parastatal oil companies were used as a cover for South Africa to import embargoed oil. This has never been proven, and oil traders and shippers did not report any extraordinary tanker movements to Seychelles. Nevertheless, a senior Seychellois diplomat has confirmed that, within a couple of years of Williamson's entry into GMR, Seychelles had come to occupy a place in South African sanctions-busting networks, apparently using paper trans actions rather than physical transhipment of oil. It is noteworthy that Fiorini's former employer, ENI, developed such a system in the 1970s for selling Arab oil to Israel via front companies and paper transactions in the Bahamas, Malta and elsewhere. SASEA may also have entertained other ideas to make money from the boycotts imposed on South Africa.

A private airline which inaugurated a weekly service from Nairobi via Mahe to Singapore, Ligne aerienne seychelloise, included at least one shareholder with close links to SASEA. It was planned to join this to a Botswana Seychelles link. Among SASEA's acquisitions was a dummy company registered in Seychelles' offshore facility called the Seychelles International Bank, which Fiorini often called SIBANK and which appears to have developed from the earlier Roberto Memmo Investment Banking. The Seychelles International Bank did not have a full banking licence and, indeed, hardly had a physical existence. Fiorini transferred the bank's official head quarters to Switzerland, although such transactions as it carried out were actually performed from a small, shabby office in Monte Carlo. SASEA issued cheques on the bank in an effort to buy shares in an Italian insurance company. Fiorini went from strength to strength for as long as he enjoyed the patronage of leading Italian politicians.

Through a series of companies, Fiorini, together with a partner, Giancarlo Parretti, who had only a few years earlier been convicted of fraudulent bankruptcy, eventually suc ceeded in a major business coup, acquiring the Hollywood film company MGM-United Artists for the sum of Sl ·3 billion, after they had earlier been frustrated in an attempt to purchase the French film company Pathe. These acquisitions were made with massive loans from the Netherlands subsidiary of the French state-owned bank Credit lyonnais. A French parliamentary commission of inquiry in 1994 failed to reveal any sound commercial reasons for the size of Credit lyonnais' lending to such dubious financiers as Fiorini and Parretti. The commission's rapporteur, a deputy from a party opposed to the French Socialist Party which then held the French presidency, gradually put together a picture of political influence-peddling linking SASEA, Fiorini and Parretti with Socialist politicians in Paris, where Parretti had been the accredited representative of the Italian Socialist Party, Rome and even Spain. Using Credit lyonnais Bank Nederland loans, the two Italians acquired a cinema chain in Britain and the Netherlands on behalf of the Italian media tycoon (and later prime minister) Silvio Berlusconi. They consistently managed to engineer major acquisitions not only with loans from Credit lyonnais Bank Nederland, but also from their own Seychelles International Bank. For the MGM acquisition they also appear to have been supported by letters of credit issued by the Sovereign Order of the Coptic Catholic Knights of Malta. Seychelles International Bank was at the heart of Fiorini's ·and Parretti's finances. where it acquired its funds from remains unclear.

SASEA was eventually to go bankrupt with debts of 2·7 billion Swiss francs, about Sl billion. Tracing exactly what happened to this money will probably be no easier than it was in the case of the Banco Ambrosiano. Credit lyonnais was left with ownership of MGM-United Artists, probably worth considerably less than what Fiorini and Parretti had paid for it, and with a loss of 6·9 billion French francs on its 1993 accounts, much of it stemming from the bad loans incurred by Credit lyonnais Bank Nederland. It appears that Fiorini and Parretti, having learned their trade in Italian political finance and enjoying excellent relations with leading members of the Italian Socialist Party, had gone some consider able way to extending the Italian system of political financing to other countries, notably France, although this is a matter which requires further investigation.

The US connection

Some influential figures in the US, too, had formed an opinion of the ease with which the Seychelles' government could be swayed and of the influence enjoyed in the islands for some years by Mario Ricci.

US security and foreign policy in the early 1980s was a bone of contention not only between competing bureaucracies-at the White House, the State Department, the CIA and the National Security Councilut also a myriad of unofficial interests loosely attached to the political entourage of President Ronald Reagan and his

Director of Central Intelligence, William Casey. This was the tangle which was to produce the Iran-contra affair, which came to public attention in 1986.

As CIA director from 1981 to 1987, William Casey actively supported a network of unofficial contacts which, in his view, would assist in the ultimate aim of securing US security interests in the world. He enjoyed the unusual status for a Director of Central Intelligence of having cabinet rank and, in the opinion of some, he was to become the most important figure in the Reagan administration second only to the President hirnse!f. Casey was an old intelligence hand who had served in the Office of Strategic Services (OSS), the forerunner of the CIA, in the Second World War. A visceral anti-communist, he took up the post of CIA chief determined to restore America's capacity to fight its foes around the world which, in his opinion and that of many in the Republican Party and in the CIA itself, had been undermined by misguided efforts, particu larly under President Jimmy Carter, a Democrat, to impose restrictions on the Agency.

This, thought Casey, had had a disastrous effect on the CIA's effectiveness and morale. Casey and other Cold Warriors in the Reagan administration encouraged an array of informal contacts to build a private-sector network which could deliver help to America's friends and allies around the world without having recourse to what they considered the emasculated CIA or the fickle, Democrat-dominated, US Congress. The revelation of illicit deals with Iran and the Nicaraguan contras was eventually to expose the existence of other secret wars fought by Casey and the CIA extending to parts of the world other than Iran and Nicaragua, and arms-dealing links with South Africa. ° Casey's basic purpose was to get money and guns to any of America's allies who needed them in order that they might inflict damage on America's enemies, and principally the Soviet Union and its allies. The South African government clearly came into the Cold War category of friends of America. It was a bastion of anti Communism in Africa and it was the main conduit to the UNITA organization in Angola.

Just as South African anti-communists saw the strategic possibilities offered by Seychelles, so did some in America. Some of Casey's associ ates, notably in the influential World Anti-Communist League, became interested in the islands, encouraging propaganda against its Socialist government, depicted in a series of articles in the US and British press in the early and mid-l 980s as a Soviet client, and fraternizing with the exiled opposiuon. In the wake of the 1983 US invasion of Grenada, it was not unrealistic to imagine the US government, or at least William Casey's fellow-travellers on the extreme right, backing a coup in strategically important, and allegedly Marxist-dominated, Seychelles.

The US Department of Defense was concerned about the Seychelles' government's pro-Soviet tendencies and had its own connections to Defence Minister Ogilvy Berlouis, who was received at the Pentagon in 1985. It appeared that some in the US security establishment saw Berlouis as a potential future president of the islands, recognizing in him an ambitious man with no ideological baggage despite his tenure of a senior post in the Rene government. The coup plan aborted in August 1986 (described above) had the active support of the South African intelligence services and claimed support from prominent U anti-communists and from the British secret services.

Perhaps the greatest controversy surrounding the Iran-contra and associ ated networks was the precise role played by the two senior members of the US executive, President Ronald Reagan and Vice President George Bush. The latter was a former Director of Central Intelligence and, unlike Reagan, an expert in foreign policy. Both during the Reagan admin istration and during his own presidency, Bush had to fight to deny having had any role in the Iran-contra affair or in other affairs related to the US government's covert or semi-privatized diplomacy and secret wars.

In view of this, it is noteworthy that one of Bush's closest aides became associated with Mario Ricci in Seychelles. In February 1985, a parmer in the US law firm used by Mario Ricci, former US Deputy Trade Secretary David R. Macdonald, travelled to Seychelles to discuss with Ricci and President

Rene how the Seychelles government could best be represented in Washington. He then discussed the matter with Vice President Bush's press secretary, Peter Teeley. Teeley resigned his position at the White House on 1 March 1985 to open a public relations practice in the private sector. Within a week of his resignation Teeley had agreed to represent the government of Seychelles in Washington jointly with Macdonald, and the two of them undertook to introduce Seychellois ministers in Washington at whatever level they desired. The bill for these services, S6,000 per month, was not paid by the Seychelles government but by Mario Ricci personally and correspondence concerning this lobbying arrangement was addressed not to the Seychelles' government but to Ricci personally. In the circumstances, it is unlikely that Teeley would have resigned a senior position in the White House to take on this consultancy without informing his employer, Vice President Bush. It is testimony not only to the importance for the US government of developments in Seychelles at that time but also to the influence which Mario Ricci was acknowledged to have.

It seems likely that senior US officials wished to cement their country's influence in Seychelles but also to outflank the more extreme anti-communists such as those of the World Anti-Communist League. Neither the South African government nor mainstream US agencies actually sought to overthrow President Rene by the mid-l 980s, and certainly not after the failed coup of August 1986, since they already had him under control. They were probably most afraid, by this time, not that Seychelles was becoming a Soviet client but that it would be destabil ized by extreme anti-communists working with William Casey. This threat from the extreme right was to disappear after exposure of the Iran-contra networks in America and after South Africa had aborted the 1986 coup. The ending of the Iran-Iraq war was later further to reduce the sensitivity of the western Indian Ocean.

American and South African interests in Seychelles were quite similar. The various arms of the US security establishment were generally agreed on the need to support the Pretoria government in the context of the Cold War, although it was not politically acceptable for Washington to state its support for the apartheid government in Pretoria unequivocally. There were also more complex aspects to this relationship. The US and South Africa were both on the same side in the Angolan war, and needed to cooperate in the supply of UNITA. In the Middle East, the US was determined to prevent an Iranian victory in the Iran-Iraq War and was supplying massive quantities of arms to Iraq but was also arming Iran in secret in order to secure the release of US hostages in Lebanon. Since the South African weapons industry was selling weapons to Iraq and being part-paid in Iraqi oil,the Americans had an interest in monitoring the flow of weapons from Pretoria to Baghdad so as to ensure the desired strategic balance between the two Middle Eastern rivals. At the same time Washington did not wish to disrupt Pretoria's oil supplies from Saudi Arabia and other Gulf states which supported Iraq in the Gulf War. As Indian Ocean islands, Seychelles and the

Comoros stood in the middle of the sea-lanes and air-routes carrying weapons from South Africa to the Gulf and oil in the opposite direction.

Some effects in Seychelles

As bureaucrats and businessmen hammered out these strategic arrange ments in offices in Washington, Geneva, Pretoria and elsewhere, and in business meetings in hotels all over the world, and as vast amounts of money changed hands, an atmosphere of intrigue and skulduggery settled on Seychelles and among some Seychellois exiles. There were occasional political assassinations or 'disappearances' in the islands, which although few in number, had an unsettling effect in such a small community. Gerard Hoarau, the most effective of the Seychellois exiles, published a series of detailed, well-documented and highly embarrassing allegations concerning corruption by the Seychelles government and promised further revelations which were never forthcoming: in November 1985, Hoarau was machine-gunned in a quiet London suburb. His killer, apparently a professional assassin, was never identified.

There were constant rumours that the islands were being used for heroin- and currency-trafficking. In late 1984, in the US, the New Jersey police found the mutilated bodies of two local drug-traffickers, apparent victims of a gangland killing. One of the two had in his pocket an address book which contained the name and address of Florio Fiorini and the name and private phone number of President France Albert Rene. The circum stances in which he had come to write these numbers in his address book were a mystery. The US ambassador to Seychelles at the time recalls that when he gave this information to the President, Rene went pale with apprehension. It was the only time that the ambassador recalls seeing Rene truly startled. Important international crime syndicates seem to have infiltrated much of the region: in London Francesco Di Carlo, a Sicilian convicted in 1987 of heroin-trafficking on behalf of a mafia crime family in a major trial, was shown to have regularly visited Mombasa, Kenya, where some casinos were said to be used by the Italian mafia for both money-making and money-laundering on a significant scale. Between the inception of Seychelles' private offshore tax haven in 1978 and 1992 some 40 companies registered to make use of the facility. According to Finance Minister James Michel, speaking in 1995, some of them 'have been engaged in illegal activities and were being investigated by Interpol and the US State Department'. In a court case in France in 1986, for example, it emerged that a company registered in the Seychelles' offshore facility had been used to trarisact major arms deals, possibly in an effort to acquire nuclear material for Libya.

Finance Minister James Michel's acknowledgement in 1995 of the abuses of the Seychelles' tax haven and measures taken by him to reform the way in which the system worked do not signal an end to the islands' involvement in money-laundering. In November 1995, the Seychelles national assembly amended the constitution in order to open the way for legislation guaranteeing immunity from criminal prosecution for any foreign businessman investing a minimum of S10 million in the islands. The Economic Development Bill provides immunity from prosecution for all investors meeting these requirements 'for all criminal proceedings whatsoever except criminal proceedings in respect of offences involving acts of violence and drug trafficking in Seychelles'. The director of Britain's Serious Fraud Office commented that it was 'the perfect present for drug barons, fraudsters and money launderers'.

The Cold War and global corruption

The fact that South African secret servants, Italian businessmen and others were able to exert such pressure on the government of Seychelles, and indeed the influence which these people had in their countries of origin, should be considered in the context of the Cold War. It was the perception of a total onslaught against the government in Pretoria which led South Africa's politicians and secret services to adopt increasingly ruthless measures throughout the region and, as we have seen, these entailed a rapid escalation of corruption in South Africa itself. The same was broadly true of Italy, for the growth of corruption in Italian public life was directly connected to the fear in certain high circles of the Italian Communist Party coming to power in Rome.

Organizations like P-2 were pledged to assure that this would not happen, and they were able to commit all manner of crimes, including massive corruption, in the name of anti-communism. For four decades Italian businessmen and voters and Italian politics itself were hostages to this system. It is no coincidence that the end of the Cold War was to encourage an extraordinary wave of political reform not only throughout Africa, including both Seychelles and South Africa, but also in Italy, where magistrates were at last able to indict politicians and others suspected of corruption.

Corruption on this scale, once entrenched, is hard to eliminate. A good example of this is provided by the maze of companies and organizations set up or acquired by the South African intelligence and security officers in their fight to defend apartheid.

Front companies established by intelli gence operatives are difficult to trace and difficult to close, not least since their existence may be quite legal and their formal ownership may be no longer vested in the state, but in nominees who cannot legally be dispossessed by administrative decree. Such companies are capable of transforming themselves, ifnecessary by acquiring a new name but continu ing in the same business, as a snake sheds its skin. In this way the arrangements made in or concerning Seychelles in the 1970s and 1980s have produced a longer-lasting infrastructure of personal connections and institutions designed to evade national laws and to perform illicit transactions.

There is evidence that illicit trade arrangements set up in southern Africa originally for military reasons survive in the form of net works engaged in the ivory, currency, diamond, drug and weapons trades. These trades have now become a major threat to the security of South Africa and they are an important feature of the political economy of various regions of Africa. This legacy is complicated by the fact that secret service and special forces operatives who have acquired expertise in covert operations have shown themselves capable of using their skills to mount totally independent ventures in the private sector. There are many exam ples of this, but an important one for the present discussion is the

South African security company Executive Outcomes Ltd. , which has worked in Angola, Sierra Leone and elsewhere and which has generated a wide array of front-companies in fields from air transport to video production. In a similar vein, successive companies manipulated or controlled by Italian political financiers have shown a similar tendency to resurface in new forms. In general, the Cold War encouraged the development of relations between crime, politics and intelligence activity, largely because secret services and politicians who purported to be acting for the greater good of the West were prepared to tolerate or even to promote politicians of dubious morality and to do deals even with professional criminals, particu larly in the Third World but also in the industrialized world. The longevity of the Italian mafia and the growth of the world narcotics trade are both in part consequences of bargains made by Western politicians and secret services with foreign governments or even with criminal elements in their own countries and sustained over considerable periods of time. The growth of transnational crime and of the corruption associated with it, often seen nowadays as an emerging security threat to the nations of the West, grows out of the Cold War itself.

If a government or an individual politician in an African country is offered unaccountable funds by foreign governments, and is made to understand that refusal can entail violent attempts to overthrow the govern ment, it becomes more understandable why some politicians may come to see international politics as a jungle, in which richer governments ruthlessly pursue their perceived national or factional interest at the expense of smaller and poorer ones. Not all African governments are subject to the same pressures as those applied to Seychelles, but there are certainly many blandishments and threats which are never publicly reported and are not assimilated in academic analyses of corruption and governance. In the cas of Seychelles, and no doubt in many other cases also, many of the pressures or promises offered from abroad were articulated by various secret services.

While there is an enormous literature and an array of specialist journals on secret services, academic studies of intelligence and security services have devoted little attention to Africa in general, with the partial exception of South Africa. The evidence of the present study suggests that intelligence services play an important role not only in the politics of some Afrian states but also in relations between rich countries and Africa and that, not surprisingly, they are often charged with the more delicate or less acceptable tasks of diplomacy. If the case of Seychelles is anything to go by, intelligence services in developed countries are largely concerned with carrying out aspects of foreign policy which are to be concealed from the domestic public rather than any other function.

If this observation is correct, the inferences which follow apply at least as much to the wealthier nations of the world as to African governments. And if analysis of the activities of major intelligence agencies in Africa tells us something about·the nature of governance in some of the world's older and wealthier democracies, it also tells us something about the nature of the political enterprise in those same democracies. Much of the unorthodox or illicit financial activity in Seychelles directly or indirectly was connected with the funding of political parties or individual politicians.

This was so not only in the case of funds used for Seychelles' own ruling party, but also in regard to Italy. SASEA's extraordinary relationship with Credit lyonnais suggests the existence of a particular relationship with Italian politi cal parties and perhaps also with the French Socialist Party. Political parties in modem advanced democracies, it seems, are permanently in search of funds in excess of what they can obtain from domestic party members of sympathizers. The competition for political power is such that they may be prepared to seek such funds from unorthodox or illicit arrangements with business, or with their own secret services, or a combination of the two. Money can be laundered in real-estate transactions and leveraged buy-outs of the type undertaken by SASEA, in which political support is crucial. It can also be laundered in some circumstances through the media industry, and here the attempts of Florio Fiorini and Giancarlo Parretti to buy film companies and newspapers meshed with the interests of politicians in acquiring influence with the media. Media magnates-cum-politicians such as Silvio Berlusconi are products of this tendency.

In as much as Africa is a field where the governments of powerful countries can pursue factional or personal interests virtually unchecked, Africa may be a more significant factor in the politics of some Western countries than is generally imagined, due to the relative ease with which unaccountable funds can be obtained or laundered there. The globalization of capital movements makes it all the easier and more tempting to carry out such transactions abroad, and here small and easily manipulable states like Seychelles are an obvious attraction. Political job-men and money-launderers come into contact with professional drug-smugglers, and streams of business, political and criminal finance may merge. Africa's role in the international narcotics trade, we may note, is increasing rapidly, not as a producer but as an intermediary for products consumed in North America and Europe. In this way problems of political funding, crime and governance more generally in the rich world become inseparable from related problems in Africa itself. The networks thus established may become independent of their political instigators, creating power blocs with enduring interests which survive changes of regime in, for example, Rome, Paris or Pretoria. The impression gained by the French Member of Parliament Franois d'Aubert, chairman of the Anti-Mafia Commission of the French National Assembly and rapporteur of the Commission of Inquiry into Credit lyonnais, is worth citing as a description of the nebulous political-financial networks in modem democracies: I observed a shadow area, a zone of contact between legality and illegality, between the licit and the criminal, between clean money and dirty money, between honest people and out-and-out crooks. It is a no-man's-land domi nated by a demi-monde of intermediaries of every kind, of corrupters and corrupted enjoying complete impunity for laundering money in investments which arc clean, safe and profitable.

In South·Africa, the growth of political corruption was associated with a very special factor, namely the protracted struggle to defend apartheid. South Africa and southern Africa may feel the effects of methods used in the service of the total strategy for years to come as Pretoria's former secret servants continue their careers either inside or outside the public service. Trans-border trafficking of drugs and weapo is frequently seen by commentators, and by the South African government itself, as a major security threat in an age, and in a part of the world, where conventional wars between states seem to have become obsolete and to have been replaced by armed conflict carried out by factional interests, often associ ated with international trades in illicit products, including narcotics. Funds gained from enterprises of this type can be channeled into political finances, and in South Africa, as in Italy and elsewhere, the dividing lines between secret services, organized crime and political parties may be seen to have become blurred to a considerable degree.

In much of tropical Africa, the decline of state power in recent years has resulted in the emergence of networks of long-distance trade in high-value commodities including gems, weapons and drugs which are both sources of wealth and vectors of political-military conflict, such as in Liberia, Angola, Somalia and elsewhere. This is an important development in which anti-corruption or good governance campaigns are of little relevance, since either these trades are outside the control of collapsed states, or the political powers which are emerging depend on them for their own finances. Such long-distance trades are producing new patterns of politics in Africa in which secret services or privatized security organizations like Executive Outcomes are playing an important role. There are examples of major banks which launder drug-money and facilitate more traditional forms of corruption such as bribery and capital flight for governments and for individual clients but which are also tolerated by major Western intelli gence agencies which find it convenient to observe, but not to denounce, the illicit flows of financing for states, drug barons, political parties and terrorist organizations. BCCI, the Bank of Credit and Commerce International, whose collapse marked the biggest bank failure in history, is the best-known example. The. detailed reconstruction in the present article may serve as a contribution to a deeper understanding of the origins and nature of these contemporary phenomena which are inextricably associated with general questions of governance and politics.

Lightning Source UK Ltd.
Milton Keynes UK
UKHW020640040321
379777UK00010B/661

9 781715 548810